Familiar Strangers

Chronicles Of Indoctrination, Liberation and Self-Discovery

Mollie Innocent

Familiar Strangers

ISBN: 978-0-9896281-0-5

Library of Congress Control Number: 2013946342

Published by: Struck Arrow Publishing, LLC

Edited by Ryan Evans

Cover design by Andersen Cupid

To my family, the given and the chosen,
whom have shown me the true definition of love.

PREFACE

This book is about the true story of Cassandra Baptiste, a woman who has struggled to survive through the devastating and long-lasting effects of extensive childhood sexual abuse. Her story describes struggles with her faith, issues with her self-image, the courage it took to break through the shame that kept her quiet, and the rebuilding of her life after finally exposing her abuser to her family.

Although this story is specific to Cassandra's life-events, sadly, her story is not an unfamiliar one. According to the National Center for Victims of Crime, one in four girls and one in six boys are sexually abused in the United States. Although child sexual abuse is reported almost 90,000 times a year, unfortunately, much of the abuse goes unreported, which is why it is often referred to as a "silent crime."

This story delineates many factors that attribute to the lack of reports, which include culture, the victim's guilt and self-blame, and society's reluctance to discuss disconcerting topics such as child sexual abuse. There are times throughout this book where the reader may feel disturbed, repulsed, uncomfortable and at times even confused, but understand that the author's goal is that you, the reader, may feel and have a deeper understanding of the emotions and access the thoughts that an abused child is faced with.

1

If you are a parent, sibling, neighbor, teacher, bus driver, therapist, or any member of society, I implore that you not turn your back on our children and continue to read past the discomfort, and continue increase your awareness of what is happening behind closed doors all over the country. If you are a survivor, the hope is that the words on these pages, albeit discomforting, will inspire you to seek treatment and galvanize within you an urge to speak out about what you endured.

The masked and hooded villains armed with guns on the five o'clock news are the monsters we have been trained to fear: strangers in dark alleyways, gang members, and home intruders. However, there has not been nearly enough dialogue about the familiar faces of the people who we have been taught to love and trust, who are commonly the real predators to our children.

The goal of this book is to encourage people to open their minds and open their mouths about child sexual abuse. It must be discussed by survivors, it must be taught to children, and it must not be a topic that society shies away from. One victim speaking out against his or her abuser may be the catalyst for ten other victims to speak up and share their stories. The hope is that this book's true and emotional story about overcoming pain and gaining strength will in turn help save at least one child from child sexual abuse. The names of people described in the story, who each played crucial roles in Cassandra's journey, have been changed out of respect for their privacy.

1

At the age of twenty-four, it feels like my life is just beginning. Even getting to this point has been a true journey. This journey, unbeknownst to me, began in my senior year of college at Rutgers University, while taking an advanced psychology seminar to satisfy my psychology major. I majored in both Psychology and Sociology and minored in Spanish. One could say that I was a bit of a nerd, taking more classes than I needed to and eventually graduating with an extra thirteen credits than was needed to obtain my Bachelor's degree. Psychology had been fascinating to me ever since I took my very first psychology class as an elective in eleventh grade.

After the first day of that class, I was so compelled by the subject that I actually took my textbook home with me and read through it as if it were a bestselling suspense novel. I was intrigued by the power of the mind over the body as I read about conversion disorders and delusions of pregnancy with physical manifestations of symptoms. I was fascinated by the tricks the mind could play, like auditory and visual hallucinations and multiple personality disorders.

That evening, I determined that when I got older, I would become a psychologist or therapist for sure. I wanted to meet these people that I had read about. I wanted to talk to them, listen to their unique experiences, work with them, and ultimately help them to cope with their symptoms so that they may go on to lead fruitful and healthy lives.

A career in psychology was a perfect fit for my personality. I was the type of person who would go to the mall and people-watch for hours—observing them interact with one another, wondering where they came from and where they were going. I was a people-person, which allowed my friendships to go beyond the limitations of typical high school cliques. I was friends with nerds, cheerleaders, athletes, and thespians. I walked through the halls with a smile, greeting people as I passed. My peers often came to me for advice, confiding in me to keep their secrets. And I kept them, although it was rare that I allowed them to return the favor. I would seldom share any stories about my own personal life, so it came naturally to listen and provide my own observations and feedback.

Four years later, I sat in one of my last college-level psychology courses, just as intrigued by psychology as the first day I laid my eyes on my eleventh-grade text. The class was small and intimate. It was a seminar and did not have a "typical classroom feel" to it, which I enjoyed. We sat at a round table weekly to discuss various topics; it made me feel more like an adult than a student.

It was in this class that I was required to make a genogram, or "family tree," which is often used by medical professionals and therapists. While completing the assignment, I pondered if I should continue to do what I have always done to keep my life simple: portray the classic family picture of a mom, dad, son and daughter.

Of course, the alternative would be to portray the truth: the father that I knew was not my biological one and my brother was in actuality my half-brother, a detail which even he had no knowledge of. For some reason, I felt comfortable enough revealing that piece of information to the class, which went against my typically guarded nature. Perhaps it was the class setting, or because I was already struggling internally with the decision to tell him the truth.

I never knew my biological father. All I know is that he was present in the hospital when I was born, and when I was about four years old, I ended up as the flower girl in my mom's wedding to another man—the only man who I have ever called "Dad."

When I was in elementary school, at recess, my classmate asked, "Cassandra, why do you have a different last name than your brother?" It was the first and only time that my brother and I went to the same school together. He was in kindergarten, and I was in fifth grade. I stopped and composed the most logical response that could be expected from a ten-year-old child. "I don't know," I said. "My last name Pierre is the same as my dad's first name"—which technically was accurate.

Nonetheless, I wasn't fully satisfied with that answer. My classmate's question stuck in my head as I rode the bus home from school. Both my brother Troy and stepsister Sorelle had the same last name, so why was I different? My stepsister, who was only one year older than me, lived with her mother in Maryland, yet she still had my dad's last name. So as any curious fifth grader would do, I asked my parents for the "right" answer. They initially told me that they would answer my question later. In hindsight, I realize that was so they could discuss and decide which answer they would agree to provide me.

A few hours later, Dad called me into his room, using the firm voice that he typically used when he was ready to commence a lengthy lecture.

"Cassandra!" he yelled from his room, elongating the vowel sounds in my name.

I cautiously presented myself, and Mom directed me to sit down. I replayed the events of the day, trying to figure out if I had done anything worth getting in trouble.

My parents sat on one side of the bed, as I sat on the other. My mother was dressed in her nurse clothes: green scrub pants and a white v-neck top with a pattern of doodles printed on it. Her hair was pulled back in a ponytail that sprawled out like the leaves of a palm tree as she leaned against the headboard. Usually Dad was the one who gave the lectures, so it startled me when she started to speak.

"Cassy, the man sitting in front you is not your real—I mean—biological father." She spoke slowly. "Your biological father isn't a part of your life," she said. "But luckily, Pierre has been here to be your dad."

My eyes quickly shifted to Dad, and I observed him as if I had seen him for the very first time. He sat on the edge of the bed. He had a small afro and was in his work clothes, a button-up shirt and khaki slacks. He looked at me but didn't say a word.

"Do you understand, Cassandra?" Mom asked.

I nodded.

She continued, "Now, this doesn't change anything; things will be *exactly* as they have always been—Pierre and I love you, and he is your dad."

Oddly, it didn't faze me at all. It was mildly shocking, but I remember being more relieved that I didn't have to sit through a lecture and that I could run along to play. I thought: *Oh well. I've only known him as my dad, so he's my dad.* It was that simple, and I didn't give it much thought afterwards.

When I got older though, I would sometimes stare at myself in the mirror, using my imagination to try and guess what my biological dad might've looked like. I had no photos to go by, and I always felt that I looked different from the rest of my family, like I didn't belong. My forehead was larger and rounder, my nose was more pointed, and I couldn't say for sure that I had my mom's eyes. I couldn't help but think about the man who fathered me.

In the eighth grade, I was legally adopted by my stepdad. It turned out that my biological father—who had previously refused to sign papers relinquishing guardianship—had passed away, thus giving my stepdad the opportunity to legally adopt me.

I remember sitting at a large round table in a room with official-looking strangers. There were three white men present, two in dark suits and ties, and the one closest to me was a chubby, balding man in a black robe. I sat nervously in my seat, fiddling with the hem of my best Sunday dress, which my mother had picked out for me to wear.

Everyone around the table was smiling and staring at me. Their smiles brought me no comfort. I had been provided simple instructions to be polite and to answer any questions I was asked at this very important meeting. I looked down at my reflection in the shiny wood table.

The heavyset man, presumably the judge, asked, "Do you want this man to be your father?"

"Yes," I replied with a nervous smile, "He's my dad." It was an easy question. He was the only dad I had known.

The judge smiled as if he was pleased with my response and proceeded to sign some papers. The adults opened their briefcases and began talking amongst themselves. My parents smiled proudly at me.

I have a picture of my mom, dad, my brother and I in the living room, smiling on the day of my adoption. I was holding a rose, given to me by my now adoptive dad. It was a day of celebration, and my brother was smiling ear-to-ear without the slightest clue as to what was going on. As an eight year old, he was just happy to celebrate something. I felt happy, feeling that now I was actually a legitimate part of the family, and I had a new last name to match. I went from being Cassandra Pierre to Cassandra Baptiste; it had a nice ring to it. My brother was too young to question the name change, and for some time, he simply referred to me as "Cassandra Pierre Baptiste."

In my psychology seminar years later, the discussion about roots and family played an integral role in my decision to finally tell my brother the truth. I believed that such information should come from our parents, yet I felt that as his best friend and older sister, he would feel betrayed if it didn't come from me. Besides, he was seventeen years old; if they hadn't told him already, they were never planning to.

I had originally made the decision to wait to tell him; however, the next time I saw him, keeping the truth from him was like damming a river with my lips. I was taking him to our favorite little pizzeria. I said, "I have something to tell you, but I really want to wait until you're eighteen first."

Troy looked confused. He replied, "What's going to change between now and a couple months from now?"

He had a point; I was trying to find an excuse to delay telling him.

So I told him. I told him in the parking lot of a pizza place with a hot pizza box in my lap.

"Dad isn't my dad," I said.

He recoiled. "*What?*" His dark eyebrows furrowed and sank like a shipwreck.

"Your dad isn't my dad."

"I mean—I heard you. It's just..."

His eyes met the floor, and after some silence, he looked at me and asked, "So you're my half-sister?"

I felt those words sting the instant they left his lips. I wasn't his half-sister. I was his sister. Period.

I said, "Just because we don't have the same dad doesn't make me any less your sister." I feared that this piece of information would alter our relationship forever. He must've sensed my panic.

He looked me in the eyes and said, "You'll always be my sister, no matter what."

I felt my heart melt as I let out a sigh.

"Great," I said. "You mean I'm stuck with you *forever*?"

We laughed, and then we ate pizza.

Back at school, a few lessons had passed since the genogram exercise, and we were now studying the uncomfortable topic of child sexual abuse. When you go to graduate school for social work, you are taught to be conscious of your body and your facial reactions so that you don't influence or affect a client with your own visceral response. As it turned out, I had already mastered this skill even before obtaining my bachelor's degree.

During the topic of sexual abuse, I would press down on the floor with my toes or tightly cross my legs to the point of having almost no circulation to my groin area. Meanwhile, my face was as emotionless as stone.

My sexual abuse was something I never thought about; it was something pushed so far back in my mind that it almost didn't exist. If the thoughts ever dared to climb to the surface, like the magic of an etch-a-sketch, I would make them disappear as fast as they came. Yet, the feeling of discomfort was something I could never manage to overcome, and there were times when it clawed at my mind like an exile with nowhere else to go.

Unfortunately for me, while listening to my professor lecture on play therapy, my childhood babysitter popped into my mind. Once he was there, no matter what I did, the memory of him remained, like a tick latched on to my conscious.

My babysitter was an old man named Mr. D, who was a good friend of my grandfather's. He was usually responsible for picking me up after school when my mother could not, or watching my brother and me when my parents had to run errands. Mr. D. had a very unusual habit, which made him different from the other adults I was accustomed to. He carried around a tin container of tobacco, and occasionally he would open it, pinch a small amount of tobacco between his fingers and proceed to stuff the brown strands into his nostrils. He carried around a handkerchief covered in brown tobacco stains, and he wore large, thick glasses and dentures that would pop out of his mouth sometimes when he spoke. He had a specific odor, like a heavy musk of tobacco mixed with the stench of bad breath.

When I lived in Philly, my brother and I would go to Mr. D's house while my parents were at work on the weekends, and sometimes after school. He was the one entrusted to babysit us. Often my brother and I would sit and watch TV in his living room on his plastic-covered couches. One time, he called me over to where he usually sat, in a chair in the dining room area that faced the TV, and asked me to sit on his lap, which I obediently did.

He proceeded to put his hand in my panties.

I froze. Every muscle in my body was stiff—literally petrified. I didn't know what was happening. I didn't know what to think. I didn't know what to do, but I wouldn't dare turn around to look him in his face. Instead, I looked dead ahead to the room where my brother innocently watched his cartoons. I imagined myself sitting there, next to my brother, lost in the TV show. It was as if I had separated from my own body.

These memories came with feelings of disgust and shame. Instead, I tried to think of something else, anything else. But my mind was immensely focused. I was in a class filled with students, and yet felt so alone. I wondered: *why did this happen to me? How can an old man be so perverted? How can you trust someone with your children, not knowing if that person is sick in the head or not?*

I could no longer focus on the words coming from my professor's lips. My mind, seemingly out of my control at this point, flashed to another occasion. It was while my family was in the process of moving from Philadelphia to New Jersey. The house was empty except for a few boxes. I was playing with my brother, and Mr. D called me into the kitchen, which at that point contained nothing but the empty china cabinet and one kitchen chair on which he was seated. He lifted me up by my armpits, put me on his lap, and proceeded to fondle me while my brother was playing in the next room.

It was happening again. I zoned out. I stared into the distance, imagining again that I was playing with my brother, imagining that I was not in the kitchen and not on this old man's lap. I daydreamed about life in my new house. I was told it had an in-ground pool with a slide and diving board, which

I imagined splashing in with my brother. Then Mr. D put his tongue in my ear and made sounds while the empty shell of my body sat there. In my mind, I was a professional swimmer doing laps around my new pool.

When he was finished, instead of going back to play with my little brother, I went into the next room and played quietly by myself. My brother came up to me, wanting to play, but I didn't want to be bothered. I felt disgusted, ashamed, and confused. I didn't know why he was doing these things to me. He was a grown-up and I was supposed to listen to him, but what he did had made me uncomfortable. Nonetheless, I felt relief knowing that it couldn't happen anymore because we would be moving far, far away.

2

My professor's voice came back into focus. I sat in my psychology seminar with my body tensed and my legs tightly crossed, playing the role of an engaged student with no personal connection to the topic at hand, child sexual abuse. It was in that classroom that I learned the statistic that would continue to haunt me for years: one in four girls in the United States is sexually abused.

I was aghast. My feelings were mixed. I felt somewhat relieved to know that there were so many others out there that could understand me and had been through what I had gone through. I was also infuriated, as I wondered why there were so many others. "One in four" did not sit very well in my stomach; it was sickening and lingered in the air like Mr. D's musk.

When I went back to my on-campus apartment, I shared with my roommate, who was also my best friend, my feelings about what I learned in class that day.

"Someone you know may have been sexually abused," I said.

Such a statement, ladies and gentlemen, is "a Cassandra test" in classic form. I'm a tester. Ever since I can remember, I would test people and gauge their reactions to see if they could handle what I had to say. Based on their reaction, I would censor myself, bend the truth, or give a bold-faced lie. As much as I don't like admitting it, I'm not one to trust others.

But you couldn't tell based on my personality.

I have always been one of those people who strike up conversation in the elevator, who will stop to give you directions, and who will approach a guy in a bar because I think he's cute. However, I also happen to be one of those people who keep others at arm's length—with fences up, alarms on, and padlocks and chains on my door. Those who have crossed paths with me would describe me as a forever-smiling, enthusiastic and energetic young lady, but they couldn't tell you anything more in-depth than that.

So with that said, how did my roommate, Brianna, become my "best friend?" Before I explain her story, let me share a bit about the "best friend" before her, Tania.

Tania lived around the corner from me. She came from a West-Indian home and understood the extreme strictness and overprotectiveness of my parents. She understood why I couldn't go hang out at the mall, for example, because of ludicrous reasoning such as "It's too dark outside."

Habitually, when I got off the school bus before my parents got home, I would go straight to Tania's house, where I felt more comfortable than at my own. Still, I wasn't allowed to sleep over at her house after years of friendship due to lack of trust and freedom from my dad, which would eventually halt further growth of the friendship as we grew older.

Regardless, Tania was closer to me than anyone else was throughout middle school and high school, but I felt she knew nothing about me. The fault wasn't hers. I perceived her as oftentimes unprepared to hear what I had to say. So with the options of keeping things to myself, bending the truth, or lying, my choices were often lying or keeping things to myself.

As far as Tania knew, I was a virgin and had only kissed a boy whom I had made-up. To other friends in high school, I had conveniently lost my virginity when others did, to a made-up boy from another school who used to write notes to me. I believe his name was Brian. It wasn't so much about me fitting in, but about making others feel comfortable.

So, how did Brianna become my "best friend?" How did she infiltrate the fences and alarms?

When I went to college, I made the choice that I would be honest from then on. I realized that nobody would ever know who I really was if I didn't give them the opportunity. Furthermore, I was no longer captive to my father's obnoxious rules, and had more freedom to develop true friendships. I figured that I would take the risk of people not liking what I had to say, and at least I would know that the friends that I made and kept would be friends who truly love me for my true self, and not just the person who makes them comfortable.

When I met Brianna, I gave her the opportunity to get to know the real me and make her own decision about our friendship. I will never forget one evening during our freshman year. I was a novice to "Thirsty Thursdays"—and to drinking altogether. As diligent students, Brianna and I had been working together on our homework for our Research Methods in Psychology class, only to be interrupted by my football player next-door neighbor who invited us to take shots of gin for a floor mate's birthday. A few double-shots later, I was plastered and passed out on my bed, only to awake hours later to see Brianna lying on my spare bed, using her coat as a blanket.

She raised her head slowly and asked, "Are you okay?"

Crisp air came through the window beside her and filled the room. I didn't know what to say. A solitary question churned in my mind like the gin in my belly, "Why are you still here?"

We had only been friends for about four months, and discovered that we lived in the same building. I was surprised that she cared about me enough to stay to ensure I was okay, when she could have easily returned to her own dorm room only a few floors up. This was a pivotal point in our friendship in which I felt that I trusted her enough to bring my guard down with her.

Three years later, as my roommate and best friend, she sat on her bed as she contemplated her response to my statement, "Someone you know may have been sexually abused." She hesitated and looked down as if to acknowledge individual threads of the carpet. Then she told me that a boy had groped her in elementary school. I was disturbed and saddened by her story. Perhaps this was an opportunity for me to tell her about mine. I wanted to empathize; I wanted to heal and to heal her. But I just couldn't. The door had been opened, but I wasn't ready to walk through.

I returned to my psychology seminar the next day, and we continued to discuss the trauma of sexual abuse. In these discussions, child sexual abuse was often paired with physical abuse or threats of violence. I got the impression that sexual abuse did not occur independently of implicit or explicit violence. I mustered up the strength to ask, "What if a child just goes along with it, without any threats of physical harm?" I was trying my best to make sure I sounded like an inquisitive student and nothing more.

I don't remember her answer, but I remember feeling lost. I felt immediate guilt. The comfort that I found in knowing that I wasn't alone vanished. I was never threatened with violence, and I was ashamed of myself for having gone along with it. And although I had been sexually abused, I didn't feel "traumatized" about it—I actually felt quite normal, which in turn made me feel worse. I felt ashamed that I wasn't the textbook child. I had not been threatened with my life or held against my will... I felt shameful for being able to function. I did well academically, I didn't act out, and I wondered to myself, *What is wrong with me?*

The course eventually ended, and I graduated with my bachelor's degree. The questions and the shame were folded up and tucked into the furthest folds of my brain, as I moved forward to the next stage of my life.

I enrolled in a master's program for social service the following year. Since I had double-majored in psychology and sociology, I felt that social work effectively encompassed the two worlds, the individual and societal. It also fulfilled my aspiration to become a therapist, and to enhance the lives of others. My program required that I do two years of fieldwork.

For my first year, I was placed in a school-based mental health program. I thoroughly enjoyed working with the children. It was a joy walking into the school and hearing excited chitter-chatter and the bustling of children as they moved from one class to the next. Their eyes looked so innocent, filled with life and energy. It brought me back to my excitement of being in elementary school, making new friends, learning new things, laughing, playing and learning.

Yet not all of the children were filled with such joy. Some children struggled with various issues, such as bullying, divorce, family problems, low self-esteem, grief, etc. One twelve-year old African American girl, one of my very first clients, served as the catalyst to the re-emergence of feelings originally stirred up two years prior in my undergraduate psychology seminar. Her name was Anya.

Anya was a beautiful young girl. She had dark chocolate skin, had a brilliantly wide smile, and wore pretty braids in her hair. She was always happy to see me. Typically, with other students, I attributed their happiness to their chance to skip class for thirty minutes to speak to "Ms. Cassandra." Some of these children did not jump at the chance to get away from academic work, because it meant talking about uncomfortable things, such as their feelings about their parents' divorce, or to work on improving their behavior. But for many, they saw it as nothing more than a get-out-of-jail-free card.

Anya, on the other hand, was the one student who would honestly tell me which classes she couldn't afford to miss. She was aiming for straight A's and didn't want to risk being taken out of classes that she wasn't on track for an A. I was immediately impressed by her honesty and scholarliness. We arranged that I only took her out of classes that she was excelling in once per week. She took school seriously and wanted very much to be successful academically. When she was not in school, she read books—and not small paperback books either. Anya would read rather thick, heavy, high-school level, hard cover books for leisure. She was mature for her age. She followed rules but had a mind of her own.

I couldn't help but smile when she shared, "People in my class always call this one kid gay. I don't think that's right. Whether he is or not it's his business and people shouldn't talk about it. And I don't see what's wrong with people who are gay. My mom's hairdresser is gay and he's really nice."

Again, I was impressed. She was a brilliant young girl. I remember after getting to know her, saying to myself, "Cassandra, meet mini-me." She was almost a replica of my personality when I was that age, and I couldn't help but have a soft spot for her.

After getting to know Anya, I asked her if she could start to talk about the reason that we had been meeting. She fell silent, but the large tears that rolled down her cheeks spoke for her. I felt a pang of guilt that I had caused this girl to cry. As a first year intern, I was actually quite terrified. Whether it was my guilt, terror, clinical insight, or instinct, I waited for her to let out her emotions. She shared that three years ago, she was molested by her mother's boyfriend, who is her baby sister's father. It wasn't until earlier that school year that she shared the information with her teacher after the memory was triggered by a statement made in class.

Her teacher had been discussing terms of endearment such as "sweetie" or "honey," and Anya started to cry. After some comforting she disclosed that those were the expressions her mother's boyfriend called her when he abused her. She then told her mom, and a court date had been set to prosecute him.

Anya struggled with fearful feelings of having to face him in court. She felt guilty because this situation had caused her mother to become distraught. Anya also became very fearful for her sister because her sister was nearing the age of seven. Seven was a cursed age for Anya, and she feared that something bad would happen to her sister at that age, the same way something bad happened to her.

I saw so much strength and courage emanating from this little girl; qualities that she didn't even realize she possessed. I found myself envious. I was envious that at the age of twelve, this little girl was able to tap into the strength inside of her to speak up, and let people know that she had been wronged. I started to ask myself, *what is it that this twelve-year-old girl has that I didn't have at her age?* As a matter of fact, I was ashamed of myself that as a grown woman I was still unable to tell anyone that I had been wronged.

"Did you know that Mr. D died?" my mom started.

"No," I replied uninterested. I was sitting across from my mom at the dining room table, collecting a small pile of crumbs that had managed to escape during dinner.

"You know, we should probably go to the funeral."

After some hesitation, I looked up to make eye contact, "Why?"

"After all of the things he did for us and our family!" She matched my gaze with an expression of shock and confusion that I would even ask such a question.

I had already gotten up and started walking away, "He sure did a lot."

This was a conversation that occurred towards the end of my senior year in college. I walked away seething, my blood at a rolling boil. How could she not know? She had to have known. What if she knew but just chose to disregard it? I couldn't believe it. I was confused, angry and sad. I played back in my head the events that took place approximately ten years prior.

After our move to Edison, New Jersey, Mr. D would some-times come to visit and would sleep on a mattress downstairs in the den. I assumed that I would be safe because I didn't think that he would dare try something while my family was in the house. I was wrong.

I quickly learned that if I were to walk into the den by my-self and he was there, Mr. D would try his best to grab onto anything he could. Knowing there were people around, I al-ways would rip myself from his grasp and go to a place in the house where I knew people were present. I picked up on the pattern of Mr. D's sneaky behavior, and I wanted to expose him for the creep he was. I devised a plan, which would provide proof. I didn't have the nerve to say out loud what he did to me without backup. He was a grown-up, and it would be my word against his. I was too afraid of the possible outcome that people wouldn't believe me, and that I might get in trouble.

I grew up in a strict, Haitian household where children are to be seen and not heard. One does not, as a child, express frustration, anger, boredom, or any negative emotions for that matter. If one was to play, it was to be done quietly, so as to not bother the adults. One should never speak against an adult. An adult is always right, and it is not a child's place to ever question one, even if the adult is blatantly wrong. Even if an adult were to admit that he or she is wrong, he or she is not required to apologize to a child, nor is it to be brought up again. One is to never interrupt an adult while he or she is speaking; whatever one has to say can wait. A child is to be obedient and respectful to all elders, without question, otherwise they were bound to get "madichon," which translates into "cursed," later in life.

But what if my elder *is* wrong? While Mr. D was in his guest area in the den, I tactfully told my brother that I wanted to play hide and seek. At this time, my brother was seven years old. As expected, he immediately jumped at the opportunity to play. I added a "special" twist to the game and convinced my brother that he was to hide in the pantry, and when he saw me, he was to jump out and scare me. I knew that through the gaps in the pantry doors, my brother could see anything that went on in the den. I had laid a trap.

Knowing that my brother was in position, I slowly walked through the den setting myself up as bait. As if on cue, Mr. D proceeded to grab me from behind, groping on my small undeveloped breasts. Just like a skit, my brother made his entrance by jumping out of the pantry, catching Mr. D off guard and causing him to jump back in shock, releasing me to run towards my brother. The deed was done. The evidence was gathered. Now, it was time to reveal the truth.

I told an adult that I wanted to share something important. I went into my brother's room, which was quiet and empty, and sat on the bed. I remember looking up at the adult's face as I explained the trap I had set and explained what my brother saw. What happened after that, I don't know. But I remember feeling very proud of myself for pulling off my plan, and finally telling someone what had happened.

Ten years later, I found myself engaging in an infuriating dialogue with my darling mother who seemed to know absolutely nothing about Mr. D's offenses—a conversation in which she was upset at *me* for lacking sympathy for the man who molested me. I was livid, not only with her for not knowing but with myself for not being able to reach into my mind for the immensely important detail of the adult's identity in my otherwise lucid memory.

After that conversation with my mom, I was driven to confirm with my brother that this memory was indeed a memory and not a hallucination. My brother confirmed that the confusing event that he experienced as a seven year old was indeed real, and that it did happen. To this day, I don't know who the adult was that I confided in over a decade ago. I don't know if my mom was fully aware yet brushed it off, if the mystery adult did not pass on the information that I shared, or if

I simply didn't articulate what happened well enough at the age of twelve.

Anya, the twelve-year-old girl in front of me, not only managed to tell her mother and teacher but also got the courts to pay attention and listen. This twelve-year-old girl inspired me. I was sad that I wasn't as brave as she was at that age.

In addition to having Anya as a client, constant classroom discussions of child sexual abuse dredged up bygone emotions. Like a slow drip from a leaky faucet, thoughts and memories that I had successfully hidden away started to flood in my mind, both while awake and while asleep. Frankly, I was annoyed, as annoyed as anyone would be when standing ankle-deep in a flooded basement. I was irritated that the deluge of unwanted thoughts and distressing emotions were arising much more frequently than I ever recalled.

These thoughts would come out of the blue, causing me to cringe wherever I was, whether it was school, work, or my internship, and I was required to employ the technique of controlling my face and body much more frequently than I was accustomed. My etch-a-sketch abilities were becoming ineffective, as these thoughts slowly began to swallow my daily activities and my mood.

I realized that in my chosen profession, I would often have to face cases of child sexual abuse. I knew if I wanted to become an effective therapist that I needed to address what was inevitably working its way to the surface before it caused me to fully unravel at the seams. I decided that at the age of twenty-four I would finally face my demons.

Towards the end of my second semester in graduate school, I looked up a therapist in the area covered by my insurance in the most logical and fail-safe way I knew how: I printed out the list of therapists, narrowed down their credentials, and picked the friendliest name of them all. After all, I used this method to find my primary care physician, and she is the sweetest doctor I have ever met. I decided to go with Donna. Donna had a Ph.D.

and I thought to myself, *Donna Teti sounds like a nice person. I don't think I've ever met a mean Donna.*

I remember my first office visit. As I walked in, I realized that depending on how this visit went, it may be both the first and last. Her office was nice and cozy. She was an older, yet stylish woman. Her short, gray hair was nicely coiffed. She wore rectangle-framed glasses and had a warm, welcoming smile. I was late, since I sped there straight from my internship, and she pointed out that I should be on time for my own benefit. I remember thinking, *I wonder if she's strict.* She sat on a leather chair and rested her legs comfortably on her ottoman. I thought, *Hmm… I guess she has no problem getting relaxed.*

The couch I sat on was comfortable, with throw pillows on it. Out of habit, I moved the throw pillow before I sat down. After working at a group home for a while, one learns to beware of pillows. (I'm sure her pillows were clean, though.) There were numerous green plants on shelves. There was a radio, which made me wonder if she played ocean sounds or relaxing music. On the end table next to her, she had a cup of coffee and a folded newspaper. Under the newspaper was a large book, telling me that she must be an avid reader. On the wall, her New York University diploma was posted. I thought, *Ah, NYU, great school. I'm sure she knows her stuff.* I provided my personal information and my insurance card. At this point, based on my assessment and positive vibes, I realized, *I'm going to keep her.*

She jotted some notes in her notepad, then handed back my insurance card. She leaned back, looked at me through her rectangular glasses, and asked, "So Cassandra, what brings you here today?"

Might as well jump, I thought.

I took a deep breath, "I am here because I was sexually abused for eight years by my father."

3

Memory: 6 years old. "Grooming"

My brother and I were in our parents' room watching TV at night. It was the weekend, and we often watched TV together. My brother and I watched from the floor. As my dad watched from the bed, my brother usually would fall asleep. He was one year old. Mom was working. She always worked weekends. I was still awake when my dad invited me up to the bed with him, leaving my brother alone on the floor.

I remember feeling so special being able to stay up late past my bedtime, plus I got to watch something scary! I loved scary movies, particularly vampire movies. *Tales from the Crypt* was on, and I remember being terrified while my dad held me. It was an episode in which a person ate something, maybe an egg, and a creature burst right out of his chest. This is one of my first memories, other than the memories of me rubbing my mom's pregnant belly, buying balloons for my new baby brother with my dad, and seeing my baby brother in the hospital for the very first time.

Memory: 6 years old. "The Beginning"

It was daytime and it was bright in the room. I don't know
where everyone else was in the house. I was wearing my favorite shorts. They were bright neon yellow with black polka
dots. I would wear them all the time. I lay in bed with my dad,
most-likely watching *Renegade*, *Knight Rider*, or a kung-fu
movie, because such were his favorites.

Without warning, my dad put his hands under my armpits,
hoisted me up, and placed my little body on his stomach. I remember feeling awkward and uncomfortable. I didn't know
why he moved me, because I was much more comfortable the
way I was before. I felt his private area against mine. My body
tensed. I turned my head towards the television and focused
really hard on what was going on in the TV show and tried to
ignore him grinding against me. I kept my body very still and
didn't make any movements, not even an inch. It was like waking up in the middle of the night and suspecting a monster to be
in the closet. You can't move, or even breathe too deep, because
that'll let the monster know that you're there, and that's when
the monster will make its move and attack.

After the TV session was over, as I started to walk out of the
room, my dad pointed out, "Oh you had an accident." I looked
down to realize that I had wet myself. He took my shorts off
and proceeded to wash them in the sink. I was mortified, waiting awkwardly, half-naked. I was too big to be wetting myself.
I hadn't even known how it happened. I was even more confused than I was before. I left the room feeling embarrassed
and ashamed. Those were no longer my favorite shorts. I never
wore them again.

The grinding episodes continued. I became less surprised
by them. I told myself that this is what happens, and I stopped
asking myself the why's of what was happening. I developed a
place in my head where I could go, which was far away from
my home. It wasn't a specific place; sometimes it was atop the

Great Pyramid, looking out over the vast desert, or beneath the rain forest canopy on some remote trail—places that I had been learning about in school. It was like stepping out of my body, and not really being there.

Memory: 8 years old. "Sex-ed"

I was hanging out in my grandparent's room with my grandparents when my father called, "Cassandra!" At that age, whenever my parents called I always wondered, *Uh-oh, am I in trouble?* I walked to his room, where he sat on his bed alone with a yellow legal pad in front of him. His face looked serious. My heart dropped as I quickly calculated in my mind what it was that I had done or not done recently to get into trouble in the past couple of days. He asked me to come close to him. I nervously walked closer, carefully putting one foot in front of the other. Corporal punishment was common in my home, whether it was a ruler to the hand or a folded belt to my rear, so I braced myself for some type of physical pain.

When I got to him, he directed me to look the yellow legal pad before him. In blue ink, he had sketched two nude bodies facing each other, one male and one female. Immediately I was embarrassed. I wasn't allowed to look at people without clothes on. I had been taught to cover my eyes if I saw people on TV kiss or take their clothes off. Nudity and shame were correlated in my brain at a young age.

He said, "This is a woman and this is a man." With his pen, he pointed to the genitals of each person, and in a stern voice said, "You should never let this, touch that. Do you understand me?"

I quietly answered, "Yes," as I averted my eyes. I thought to myself, *Isn't that what he has been doing to me when we watch TV?*

I didn't want to think about it or ask questions because I thought he might get mad. I reasoned that he must've been giving me the "talk" that all parents give their kids. I felt ashamed and didn't dare look at him in his eyes. He told me he was done, and I returned to my grandparent's room, my cheeks aflame. Luckily, with my skin complexion, my embarrassment was easily concealed.

"What did your dad need you for?" my grandma asked.

I looked down and said, "Nothing." I didn't have an answer.

Memory: 9 years old. "Daddy's Little Girl"

I had been given the title "daddy's girl." Maybe it was because in general I spent more leisure time with my dad than my mother since she was often at work. Maybe because that's what all girls were supposed to be. I was supposed to be the daddy's girl, while my brother was a momma's boy. Maybe it was his way of getting away with treating me "special." It wasn't only the nights I got to stay up past my bed-time; in the day-time I would get extra attention and affection from my dad, too.

If I asked him for something, like candy, he would give in and let me have it. He would always tell me that he would do anything for me because I was his little girl. I liked the attention and embraced the title, especially since my toddler brother, as a new member of the family seemed to always be the focus of attention. He was doing all kinds of cute things: saying new words, getting potty trained, waddling around and being over-all too cute. Furthermore, my mother seemed very happy that my dad and I were bonding well, and she cosigned the "daddy's girl" title. We were one big happy family.

Memory: 10 years old. "Movie Night"

Things changed slightly when we moved to the new house in New Jersey. My brother and I had our own separate rooms. We didn't watch movies together on the weekends anymore like we used to. My mother started to work nights, so during the day, she would be asleep. Sometimes she'd pick up extra shifts, which made her absent on the weekends as well. Instead of family movies, when my brother was out of earshot, my dad would mention, "I just got a new movie, if you want to watch it." Of course I wanted to watch a movie.

At first, he would come to my room after the house was dark and hover over me, motioning for me to follow him into his room. I figured this was so that my brother didn't get jealous that I got to stay up later than he did. He was too young to stay up as late as I did. I was getting older, so I got privileges. Every time I went, I hoped that we would just watch a movie. Every now and then, my hopes came true, but other times, it was more than a movie.

After some time, when he would ask, I learned to just walk across the hall on my own. Sometimes I really didn't want to watch a movie, but I was too afraid to say no, so I would just fake being asleep so that he wouldn't bother me. It never failed that if I did not go across the hall to his bedroom, he would open my door and say, "So, you don't want to watch the movie?"

It was evident that it wasn't a question, and I would dutifully get out from under my covers and follow him to his room.

Memory: 10 years old. "School is in Session"

As a kid, I would keep my eyes open as long as possible so that I could watch the whole movie. Typically it was past my bedtime and I was drowsy. As soon as I would start dozing off, my dad would make his move. It got to a point where he didn't even wait for me to get sleepy; he'd just turn the TV off and tell me that I looked tired.

At this stage, it had progressed beyond grinding. He would start to kiss me and explain to me, "It is a father's role to teach his daughter how to do these things. So when you get a boyfriend, you'll know how to do it well."

I accepted his explanation and went along with it. I started to wonder if this was how everyone learned how to do these things—these "things that two people who love each other do."

Either way, the feelings of embarrassment never left me. In my head, doing things in darkness, feeling that I was too young to "prepare for a boyfriend" made me feel very awkward, yet the reaction to the stimulation of my body betrayed my mind, thus causing me to feel confused and ashamed.

Memory: 11 years old. "It's My Job"

Action and horror movies turned into pornography. He would put on gritty pornographic films from the eighties or nineties and then instruct, "We should do what they are doing on the TV."

I obeyed. I had become desensitized to nudity. Conversations about sexual things became the norm. We discussed the pornographic movies like two adults would discuss a documentary. In my mind, I was mature enough to watch and discuss sex like an adult. I was unfazed. It was what I had been groomed to do.

During one of our movie nights, I was bold enough to ask, "Why don't you do these things with Mom?"

He became very silent and somber, turning away from me and saying in a low voice, "Your mom doesn't do it anymore."

I was floored. Had I taken her place?

I asked, "How long?"

"Two years." He had a melancholy expression on his face.

That night, I lay in my bed trying to process this information. Now I understood why he came after me. It was more than just a lesson. I knew that truth already buried deep inside of me, but I didn't want to admit it. It's because Mom wasn't doing her job. It's her fault that he needs to come to me. If she had fulfilled her obligations as a wife, and as a woman, then her daughter wouldn't have to be subjected to it.

At the age of eleven, I started to view my dad as a victim. It's not his fault. My mother was then moved to the shit list. It was her fault.

Memory: 12 years old. "Everyone does it"

In the beginning, after a "movie night" and my dad provided me with a "lesson," he would rush me out of his bed. I was usually drowsy since it was past my bed time; I'd just want to sleep. I didn't understand why I couldn't just leave when Mom came in the morning. He could just explain that we had a movie night, and she would just tell me to go to my own room. Instead, he would quickly gather my things and insist that I return to my own bedroom immediately, which raised my suspicions and increased the feeling that I was being "bad." As time went by, I learned to just get up and stagger sleepily to my room.

One morning, when my mom returned from work, she noticed my bra on her bed. I remember hearing her ask, "What's this doing here?" I braced myself for the wrath of my mother, but my dad must've given her some sort of answer out of earshot because my mother did not come screaming into my room. Instead, she had no reaction at all. She wasn't angry; she calmly came to my room and returned my bra to me.

This solidified in my mind that Mom knew exactly what was going on. My Dad must've been telling the truth after all. I fought my gut-feeling and figured that it was probably something that everybody does but nobody talks about. I even assumed that she must be doing the same exact thing to my little brother Troy, since he's the age when Dad started with me. I wondered when my mom did this to my brother since she worked so much. I thought that this must also mean that Tania's dad did it with her too. I almost asked Tania about it... almost.

Memory: 12 years old. "I am asking for it."

Sometimes if I caught my dad's eye when nobody else was around, he would say something like, "Oh, I know exactly what you're looking for." At first, I didn't know what he meant, because I didn't recall asking for anything. I soon came to realize that he was referring to our nocturnal activities.

Once or twice, he varied the activities by trying to put his penis into my mouth. I had seen it in the videos he had shown me but prayed that he would never do it to me. I continued to be obedient, convinced that I must've been doing something to bring this onto myself. I had never been that up close to a man's genitals before. The odor was the first thing that hit me. It was putrid, and my eyes watered. I felt the coarse hair on my small hands and started to heave. I was overcome by severe nausea and was convinced that my dinner was on its way up. I was terrified. He affectionately told me that I was not yet ready. I silently said a prayer, knowing that God had spared me.

I never found out what exactly I had been doing that made me "want it" or "ask for it." I could never figure out whether it was something bad I was doing which was causing me to get punished, or if it was something good I was doing that was getting me rewarded. Either way, no matter what, I could not escape my fate.

Memory: 13 years old. "No More Lessons"

Over the years, the sexual abuse progressed with time. It evolved from grinding while I watched TV to kissing, groping, fondling, rubbing and grinding without clothes. At the age of thirteen, my dad penetrated me. He seemed as shocked as I was about it, as if it was I who was doing something to him; he paused for a split second, giving me the impression that he would stop, but he pushed nonetheless.

I was in so much pain; it felt like my body went into shock. My body was paralyzed. My brain catapulted me to another place. I was soaring, high above where my body lay, in another universe where this wasn't happening to me.

When he finally stopped thrusting, I just lay there, frozen, not sure what to say or do. I stared at the ceiling, afraid to look elsewhere. He had no explanation this time for what he had done. No lesson to be learned, no passage into adulthood. Nothing. I collected myself and returned to my room, feeling numb. It didn't feel real.

Although I imagined myself elsewhere while it happened, I can still remember this moment as if it were yesterday: the wild look in his eyes, the sound of his wheezing, the feel of his breath on my face, and the feeling of his heavy weight crushing my tiny body. Things were different after that. The feelings of awkwardness and discomfort from the embarrassing and secretive acts before were nothing compared to the overwhelming feeling of violation.

It was a point of no return. I felt soiled. I thought, *He said he was preparing me for a boyfriend, but what boyfriend would want me now knowing that I had sex with my dad?* I think, after coming to that conclusion, I accepted the curse—the madichon—that was placed on me. I no longer questioned, I no longer reasoned, I no longer felt... anything. I became a zombie, listlessly following instructions. I had no control over the present, and no longer cared about myself or my future.

Memory: 14 years old. "Powerless"

One evening, I'm not even sure that I had agreed to a movie, or if that "question" was presented. I lay half-asleep in my bed and awoke to my father on top of me. He never ever entered my room before, but this time he was crazed, removing my clothes and proceeding to have intercourse with me. If there is a level beyond feeling violated, that's exactly how I felt. I wish I could describe what it feels like to be asleep in your own bed, a place in which there is a presumed blanket of safety, and to be awakened to a person violating the most delicate part of you. I believe, up until that point, I had the delusion that I had some sort of control over saying yes to the "movie night." I had the delusion that I had a choice. I never wanted to admit to myself that I didn't have at least that tiny bit of power. That night, I learned that I was powerless.

4

I spent weeks upon weeks talking to Dr. Teti about my college story, the history of friendships, romantic relationships, and whatever else was on my mind. I thought I was, to some extent, getting away with not talking about the sexual abuse. I figured: *Well, since I'm in therapy, I can also address all of the other issues that are going on in my life.*

The more I talked to Teti, the more I realized that the way I view myself, and the way that I view the world, has been influenced by my sexual abuse. Techniques, which I learned from a young age to survive in my house, were the same ones I applied to the world. I viewed myself as different, like I carried the mark of Cain. I saw the world as deceptive; people were not to be trusted. I avoided any feelings of pain or conflict by keeping things bottled inside. My burden was my own, and not for anyone else to carry. My feelings were less important than the comfort of others, so it was my job to appease and play the role that I was assigned.

I always reasoned that I had limited friends because it's just my style. The truth is: I am the master of getting to know you, and not letting you know me.

You are in the same class as me, and I recognize your face because I think you live in the same building as me. I would approach you and enthusiastically say, "Hey, you live in Clothier Hall, right?" We'd sit together for the rest of the semester, become friends on Facebook, and maybe even study together.

You are my co-worker. We'll talk and exchange stories every day. You may even become my favorite co-worker. We may go out to celebrate your birthday, or occasionally grab drinks and have a great time outside of work.

You live next door to me. We always talk when we're on the elevator and let each other know when we'll be throwing parties, out of courtesy to one another. We apologize if we're ever being too loud, also out of courtesy to one another.

In the end, you will always be that classmate, that co-worker, and that neighbor, but nothing more. I love people. I'll go as far as saying I'm a "people-person," which is why I entered the field of social work. I love meeting new people, learning where they're from, and where they're going. I become invested in their happiness and success. Often, I play the role of the listener and the advice-giver. People are often content with being able to have me for support and do not demand that I lean on them in return.

So why do I put out the Welcome Mat but set the security alarm and put my guard dogs out? The truth is, simply put: people are scary. People can judge. People can hurt. People can disappoint. People have ulterior motives. For me, opening up to people feels like open-heart surgery. It's like lying there, helpless, while your insides are being probed and examined by a person whom you put your trust in. You lie there, hoping that you'll come out okay, with minimal scarring. This is why I didn't trust. This is why I didn't expose.

"You don't want to be vulnerable." There goes Teti again, sitting across from me, putting into words what I didn't want to admit. Dammit, Teti. It annoyed me when she did that. At times, she could read me like a book. Nonetheless, I came to appreciate it and felt that she truly understood me.

I found it fairly easy to open up to her. Aside from my initial assessment of her outfit and office, I became aware of the safe and judgment-free environment she provided for me, allowing me to leave my guard dogs at the door. She challenged me to better understand myself. She challenged me to truly get in touch with the reasons why I do what I do, increasing my self-awareness. She then validated my feelings of fear and distrust of others. My mother fell in love with and married a man who took advantage of her daughter. The person who I trusted to be a father to me instead used his power to corrupt my innocence. I had my reasons.

Friendships to me were black and white. You were either my friend or you were not. It was all or nothing. I am only now, at twenty-four years old, just beginning to comprehend the spectrum of gray.

Let me explain Tania. Tania was my best friend in high school. After graduation, we both went away to college; she went to NYU, and I to Rutgers. I didn't mind visiting her in the city often because I enjoyed the excitement of the New York and had initially wanted to go to college there; however, Tania only visited me once in our four years of college, even though her house was less than fifteen minutes away from campus. Our phone conversations were mostly trips down memory lane, having little to do with current happenings, and were usually preluded by her apologizing for "being a bad friend" by failing to contact me. Like two continents, we were drifting apart, unnoticeable at first, yet wholly inevitable.

I received a call from her one day, and she said through heaving sobs that her father had passed away. My heart broke for her. It was a sudden and shocking loss. Subsequently, I continued to reach out and be there for my best friend. Despite the drift, I wanted provide support, a shoulder to lean on—yet at a time where I assumed that I was needed the most, I realized that I wasn't needed at all. My efforts to console were dismissed. I gave her space and time to grieve, decreasing the frequency of my phone calls, but I realized that all efforts were futile. She had whatever she needed. I had been actively pursuing a friendship which no longer existed. It took quite a while for me to come to terms with this, but after reaching out numerous times, with no response, I accepted that we were no longer friends. Such an ending to a friendship left me feeling disillusioned to others.

I made a vow in meeting Brianna; after establishing her trust, I would be truthful with her, and in time, she would come to know and understand me. In the early stages of our friendship, I would initially tell her half-truths. I would then gauge her reaction, and then days, maybe even weeks afterwards I would tell her the whole truth. I always would tell her the whole truth, even if it came in parts. Brianna came to understand this about me, and never pushed me to divulge anything I wasn't ready to. She trusted that I would come around to telling her on my own time, and she never judged.

Confiding in Brianna was a major risk for me. I had all of my eggs in one basket. In my mind, a person could only have one best friend, which caused me to put a limit to the level of intimacy that I allowed with others. I didn't understand how people could have numerous best or close friends, because the risk of being hurt multiplied exponentially with each additional friendship. Therefore, I allowed myself to take that one big risk; I could only allow all others to be acquaintances. I'd much rather have a person break my skin than give a person an opportunity to break my heart.

She was my first true friend. I remember telling her—half-jokingly, half-seriously—"You know if we ever stop being friends, I'm going to have to kill you because you know way too much about me."

Brianna was terrifically and terrifyingly close to my heart. She was the person to whom I confided my secrets and my innermost thoughts and feelings. This friendship was placed on a pedestal, so if there ever was a flaw, I would obsess over it, the way an inspector would be cautious of cracks forming in the foundation of a building. I had concerns over fluctuation in communication. I had fears of her valuing other relationships over our own. I wanted to be the first person alerted if anything ever happened, and if I wasn't, I feared that I'd been dropped to a lower standing on the totem pole.

Every single instance in which I felt possible betrayal or emotional pain, every muscle in my body urged me to escape. I told myself that it was impossible to ever trust someone to be so close. I wanted to make the slightest pain instantly go away, and I would shut down and become numb. Systematically I would try to find reasons to disassociate from her; that way, I wouldn't have to care. I wouldn't have to feel. I was hyper-vigilant to any signs that indicated that my vulnerability was in danger. I was so focused on protecting myself in the context of a close friendship that I didn't notice that Brianna was doing the same.

Brianna had asked me once, jokingly, "Are you going to Tania me?" She had turned Tania's name into a verb that meant "to cut one's friendship off." Although I was fully aware of how hard it was to come to the conclusion that my ten-year relationship with Tania had dwindled to nothing, Brianna saw the ending of a close friendship as it was happening. At first, I took offense to such a remark; it questioned my loyalty, but I later realized, with the help of Teti, that Brianna had her own fears, just like I did.

The difference between Brianna and me was that I kept my fears hidden inside. I scrutinized everything but would never express myself for fear that it would result in an altercation. It wasn't that Brianna wasn't a person I could talk to. It was more my tendency to avoid unpleasantness.

Teti challenged me to face the "unpleasantness." Either I was overreacting or I had valid feelings, and it was only fair for Brianna to be made aware of them. She helped me realize that in shutting down to avoid the bad, I was also shutting off the potential good. I agreed, and had never seen it in that way, but I gave Teti a hard time nonetheless. I wanted to earnestly make the changes, but it was going against my nature. It was as illogical to me as a deer prancing out from protective foliage where unknown peril awaits. I was adamant about leaving things be and stubbornly believed that if I had a problem, it was my problem alone and no one else's.

Why put out raw and vulnerable emotions with the risk of being hurt? No, not I. I shut down. I etch-a-sketch. I avoid. These are things that I have successfully been doing for years. These are things that I've had to do to survive in my own skin. If I got hurt, I'd bandage it up and hope the wound would heal. If I felt that I was wronged, I would bury it deep inside me to keep the peace. It was never worth bringing up, because my feelings didn't matter.

Just like they didn't matter in college. Dave, the guy who I had been intimate with; the guy who I allowed to sleep in my bed, share my closet, eat my food, who I considered a close friend, and to whom I professed my affections multiple times, had sex with my other roommate. Needless to say, it was a slap in the face with a spiked mace.

It didn't help that I woke up that morning without him next to me, became concerned, and instantly got up to search the apartment for his whereabouts, only to find him asleep in her bed. It didn't help that I had settled for a "no-strings-attached" relationship with him since he said he wasn't ready for a real relationship, only for him to have sex with my roommate. It didn't help for a person who I considered a friend of two years to do something so thoughtless and so hurtful.

My initial reaction: nothing. Even after it was confirmed a few weeks later by my roommate that they did have sex, I felt nothing. My logic: I had no right to be upset. We weren't dating; therefore, he could do whatever he wanted. He had no responsibility to me and owed me nothing. I didn't think about the fact that I had provided him with a place to stay when he couldn't afford on-campus housing, just so he wouldn't have to have a two-hour commute to and from school. I had offered him my home, my food, and my personal space because I cared about him. Yet still, I couldn't get myself to do anything about it. So I numbed myself; I wasn't allowed to feel anything.

Brianna, on the other hand, took immediate action. The moment she discovered what had happened, she went into my closet and threw all of his clothing out into the living room. Although I couldn't act, she acted on my behalf. Dave sat in the living room in shock.

I was completely overwhelmed and went down to my good friend Micah's apartment to get away. Micah was the closest male friend I had. It was the first genuine relationship I had with a man who didn't want me for my body. I took refuge in his apartment, away from the high intensity of emotions going on two floors above us.

After the blowout, my roommate continued to invite Dave into the apartment. It was implied through Brianna's actions that I had rescinded my invitation. So, I would come home after a long day of class and work, exhausted, and unable to relax because Dave and my roommate would be fraternizing enthusiastically on the couch together in the living room.

Even though they were casually hanging out, it felt like a stab to the heart seeing them together. I would spend hours of discomfort locked away in my room, as their chatter or sounds of laughter seeped underneath my bedroom door, just loud enough to be heard over my TV.

One night, I had come home slightly before midnight, after a long day of school and work, grateful that the apartment was dark and quiet. As I got ready for bed, I heard distinct moaning from the other room. Instantly, I felt a sharp pain in my abdomen and was overcome by intense nausea. I went to bed, but I didn't get any sleep that night. I never heard them having sex again, but the physical manifestations of my emotional pain intensified as months went by. My apartment no longer felt like the home it once did. I was stressed about school, work, and now, home. I chose to suffer in silence, rather than cause conflict by bringing my feelings to light and bringing distress to others.

My sleeping patterns became irregular, and I was tired all the time. I had bouts of nausea, and it felt like there was an ulcer growing larger and larger in my stomach. It wasn't until months later, after encouragement from Brianna and the physical ailments became unbearable, that I finally decided to say something to my roommate.

She expressed that she respected my wishes but that they liked each other and might even start a relationship. As she said this, my muscles began to quake. Afterwards, Brianna told me that I was actually turning red despite my dark chocolate complexion. Her words echoed in my head: "A relationship."

After all that I put up with from Dave, *she* was able to get a committed relationship after only a few months. I felt an odd combination of fury, pain, and sadness all at once. After mustering the courage to express myself, I found out that there was no way out of feeling the way I did.

Feeling irritated that expressing my frustrations got me no-where—again—I went with Brianna down to Micah's apartment to get away from it all. Three months after the initial incident, my friends looked on in shock as hot tears flooded my eyes and spilled over my cheeks down my face. I buried my face in my hands and sobbed hysterically on the couch. This was the first time they had ever seen me cry.

5

My father was two people. He was the man who helped me with my homework. He was the man who sometimes facilitated communication between my mom and me. He was the person who gave me spending money. He was the man who would have hour-long conversations with me about politics and current events. He was also the man took advantage of my childhood and me. I somehow was able to separate the two people. The morning after a movie night, I would act "normal" just like he would. The roles had changed. He spoke to me as a father to a child, and I would respond accordingly.

My boyfriend, Brian, was also two people. I dated him on and off for two years in college. Brian was the person who called me every night while I was studying abroad in Spain, wrote me poems, and would profess his undying love for me.

I had saved up a lot of my money earned throughout high school, and I always had dreams of traveling the world. So when I had the opportunity to study abroad during the summer of my sophomore year of college, I decided that I would start my exploration of the world. It was an opportunity to improve my almost-fluent Spanish, get credits for my minor, and spend three months away from my family in a foreign country. I was proud that my strong work ethic paid off and that I was able to pay for the trip all by myself, at the age of nineteen.

As much as I loved the excitement of being in a foreign country, I found myself lonely, and Brian provided me with that constant connection to something comfortable and familiar. Brian showered me with the attention that I had craved from Dave, and I was flattered to see his car littered with international phone cards when I returned to the states from my long trip.

After Spain, Brian would take me on strolls through the park, take me to nice dinners, and provide encouragement when I needed it. Yet as time passed, Brian was also the person who would remind me that he's only with me for my body and that he could always do better than me. If I caught him in a bad mood, he would curse at me and blame me for his woes. I knew I deserved more. In my mind, I knew that I was a good person, and I deserved better. Yet it took many instances of ending things with him and taking him back before I made the final decision to no longer entertain his abusive treatment towards me. It was no longer worth taking the bad along with the good.

"Your divining rod is skewed," said Teti.

"My what?"

"It's a tool that looks like a forked stick they used to use back in the day to find bodies of water. You know your worth, and you know you deserve one thing, but it seems like you're being drawn to the opposite."

As much as I suppressed the memories of my abuse, it certainly played a role in the woman I had become. I abhor the thought of myself as a victim, or the thought that I am a defect due to what has happened to me, yet it would be naïve of me to say that I could surgically remove eight years of experience from my personality and say it has had no impact on me.

With Teti, I worked towards facing my fears, learning to trust, and opening up to others. The deer's knees shook in fear.

She took baby steps, one foot after the other, towards the open plain. The bright sunlight hit her fur. It frightened her, but she hesitated long enough to feel how the sun warmed her, and that it felt good.

Emotional work, I've concluded, is far harder than physical work. I'd rather spend the entire day lifting cement blocks than spend one hour discussing emotionally difficult topics. As an intern, I would sometimes get frustrated at my clients for not getting in touch with their most difficult emotions in order to progress in treatment, but now I understood. Intentionally digging up the pain and hurt that is buried deep inside you, hurt that you have made a conscious effort to forget, is like digging up a corpse.

First you must remove six feet's worth of heavy, compressed dirt. This requires tenacity, physically unearthing soil that has grown stubborn with time. You feel sweat on your brow, and the muscles in your back and arms beg for relief as you toil through the aches and soreness. When you get to the actual corpse, it has already rotted. You want to turn your head away, but you have to look at the rotting flesh that is falling off the bone. The horrid stench of the rancid body fills your nostrils, causing your eyes to water as you fight the urge to expel all of the contents of your stomach.

The more I talked about my history, the more panicked I felt. There was a tightening in my chest accompanied by the fight or flight response that would urge me to avoid, avoid, avoid. Needless to say, I would've rather been the corpse than talk about my sexual abuse. Sometimes I would go into Teti's office and just blab about miscellaneous things, hoping she wouldn't catch me avoiding.

I'd smile when she'd eventually say, "Are you talking about this because it's important to you, or are you avoiding something else?" She was clever enough to catch my tricks.

To be difficult, I'd say, "I have no idea what you're talking about," but would ultimately succumb to discussing the true reason I was in therapy.

Sometimes, I would employ the "doorknob therapy" tactic, where I would talk about particularly difficult things with only a few minutes left of the session, with full knowledge that I wouldn't have enough time to process it. I thought I was cunning, but Teti would certainly remind me of it next time we met. Sometimes, I would actually cancel on purpose, making the excuse that I wasn't feeling well, just because I didn't want to face the difficult feelings that arose in talking about sexual abuse. I thank that woman for her patience with me.

It took me months to even say aloud what my father did to me. It was foreign to hear it aloud, coming out of my mouth. It was like entering The Twilight Zone.

Despite my connection with Teti, I never allowed myself to come to tears in her office; I'd gotten close, but I would hold back until I reached my car, when I was alone. In her office, instead of tears, there was anger.

"I'm angry at you because I never had so many unwanted thoughts before I came here," I said to Teti.

I knew it wasn't her fault, but I wasn't only thinking about the abuse on the days I went to see her. I would wake up in the morning after a dream involving my father and want to— and sometimes would—punch a wall because I was so angry. I thought about it the day before therapy, the day after, and all the days in between. My etch-a-sketch abilities were put to the test numerous times throughout the day, as I dealt with unwanted, intrusive and seemingly spontaneous thoughts.

I would be driving to work, and *FLASH* I'd have an image of my father's body on top of mine. I'd be in class taking notes, and *FLASH* I'd feel my father's breath on my neck. I'd be lying in my bed, watching TV, and *FLASH* I'd think about the time when my father violated me in my own bedroom.

Teti suggested that I write down when I did experience intrusive thoughts. Yet, the idea of actually writing down the repulsing images in my mind was unfathomable. I felt that writing it down made it far too concrete for my comfort. I often wished that it was all just a dream and that one day I would wake up and realize that I could live a "normal" life with no memories of sexual abuse. But at the very least, if it was in my head, I could make it disappear almost as quickly as it appeared. It wasn't until almost a year in therapy that I was finally able to put on paper the invasive thoughts in my mind. Even then, it was hard to shape the words with my pen.

On a regular day at my house, I'd pass by my father in the hallway and say hello. On another day, I'd pass by my father in the hallway and I'd have a different reaction. Depending on the timing, I would catch a scent of his body odor on his pajamas. There's something about having just woken up that makes one's body scent stronger in the morning—maybe it's being wrapped up in a blanket all night or just the way our bodies work. Either way, a slight whiff of his scent catapulted me back into that bed with him, with him on top of me. My body would immediately tense up. In my mind, I conjured a vivid image of me getting a knife from the kitchen drawer and stabbing him with it in the chest. I had fantasies of ambushing him with a bat while he slept, or perhaps running him over in the street with my car. Violent and gruesomely bloody daydreams were not uncommon at this stage in my therapy. Those particular mornings, I'd be ruder than usual.

Overall, I avoided my father whenever I could. I had already been disappointed that I had to return back to my house after graduating from college, but especially since I started going to therapy, being home was difficult.

Oftentimes, I would go a whole week without so much as seeing his shadow. If I had to see him, depending on the day,

I was perceived by my family as unnecessarily rude or as having an attitude problem. If I were rude to him, he would then complain to my mother about it, who in turn would reprimand me. He was manipulative and very adept at playing the victim role. As a result of his ploys to get my mom against me, I would respond angrily at her for blaming me. I hated the attacks. The issue was always me, and never him.

"What's wrong with you?" Mom often asked.

To her, I was the problem. I didn't really speak to Mom because we never had a close relationship to begin with. We only inhabited the same space. She was either at work, at home complaining about work, or at home not wanting to be bothered because she was tired from work. Even when she spoke on the phone to co-workers or friends, it was more often than not about why work was awful, and how much she hated her job.

I remember her telling me that I was foolish to think that I would find a job that I enjoyed because "everybody hates their job." My mom and I never had the kinds of conversations typical of a mother–daughter relationship. She didn't ask me how my day was or how my life was. I remember trying to strike up multiple conversations with her, but she would frequently brush me off, particularly if her soaps were on. Even when I invited her to track meets, or theatre productions I was involved in, she would respond, "I'm not interested in those kind of things."

When we did speak, it was often her reprimanding me about something I didn't do correctly. Otherwise, it would be cordial. I have memories of spending time with my mom when I was younger—standing beside her while she cooked in the kitchen, sitting between her legs while she braided my hair, teaching me how to braid my doll's hair, or walking with her to and from school or in the grocery store. As the years passed, however, those bonding moments slowly disappeared.

The only people who consistently showed affection for me were my grandma and my brother Troy.

My brother and I have always been a team, a duo. He didn't like our parents very much either, but he had his own reasons. I'm confident that if I didn't have my little brother, I'd be a completely different person. We cared about each other and spent most of our time together. I always looked after him. Others found it strange that he and I were so close. I suppose it was typical for brothers and sisters to fight, but we grew up in a household where we had only each other to lean on, and that's exactly what we did. If he was going to get a spanking, and one of our parents asked me for a belt, I would conveniently have misplaced all of mine. And if my parents asked him to divulge any of my secrets, he would refuse. We had each other's backs, no matter what, and we still do.

As for my grandma, although I don't have any recollection of the four years I spent with her as a baby in Haiti, she and I have a special connection to each other.

She has a radiant smile, and a distinct laugh where she tilts her head back and shut her eyes, letting out a hearty "hahaha." What makes the laugh unique is the "eeee" sound she makes at the end, almost as an indication that the conversation may resume. For those who don't know her, she appears stern with the deep vertical wrinkles between her brows on her unsmiling face. But it only takes a simple "hello" for her eyes to light up, and for welcoming wrinkles to materialize around her gray eyes. She is a *grimelle*, or "light-skinned" and her skin is incredibly smooth. Her hair is short, gray and curly. She was self-conscious about it thinning in the back, and often wore it in a tiny ponytail, unless she was going out. Then she would wear a wig.

What I love the most about my grandma is her energy. If she caught me doing a Tae-Bo workout, she would join in, doing what she could. I tried not to laugh at her comical movements, but she's the type of woman who can laugh at herself. She has a young spirit. She's also a religious zealot and would walk the mile-and-a-half to church if she needed to, so as to not miss her Sunday mass, which was in English. She only spoke Creole. Yet, she had a fascinating ability to make friends, using the very few phrases she knew: "God Bless You," "How are you," "I'm fine, thank you." Perhaps it was her aura, or her smile, but people were drawn to her. She was a people-person. Whenever there was a surplus, whether it was food, money or clothes, she would share it with the less-fortunate.

They say that in the first couple years of a child's life, there is a special bonding that takes place, and it seems to have taken place between my grandmother and me. As my mother put it, "I couldn't trust daycares in Brooklyn, so I sent you to Haiti." In making a decision to protect me as a child, she instead potentially hampered the growth of our relationship in the future. When I got older, my grandparents would spend the warmer half of the year visiting our family, and once it got cold, they would high-tail it back to Haiti. When they visited, my grandmother would invite me to sit with her and ask me what was going on in my life. I would sit on her bed and tell her all kinds of stories and show her pictures of what had been happening since she'd been away. She was like a best friend to me. She was sensitive to my struggles and in tune to my emotions.

My grandmother would always mention the tension that was evident in the home during her visits. One day, while my grandmother and I were in the kitchen together, she brought it up again.

"Cassandra, honey, why is it that you're not more affectionate with your parents?" she asked. This was a question that she asked at least once on every visit to our house.

Instantly irritated, I replied, "That's just the way it is grandma. Why do you always bring it up?"

Her voice filled with sadness as she said, "It breaks my heart to see the family like this. A family should be more loving than this. You should be able to show your father the same affection that you show me."

I knew my grandmother was aware that she ranked higher than my parents did in my eyes, and for that she felt guilty and wanted to make things better between my parents and me. I started to become angry. I didn't want to talk about it. It was hard for me to shut her out, because I knew that she was coming from a place of genuine concern. Had it been my mom's typical accusatory approach of posing the question, I wouldn't have even entertained it and would've walked away as I had done countless times in the past.

Exasperated, I said, "Grandma, there are reasons why things are the way they are, and that's just the way it is."

The wrinkles of her brow deepened with thought. Then she said, "What did he do to you, Cassandra?"

Unlike my mom who always assumed that I was the problem, my grandma's sincere question pointed to the possibility that my father was the problem. I had my back to her as I was peeling hard-boiled eggs in the sink. In my mind, I had a vision of sudden logorrhea in which I told my grandma everything that he did to me, from the beginning to the end. I imagined spewing all of the details in an emotional explosion, like hot water bursting from a geyser, feeling an instant release from the pressure building up inside of me. Instead, I shut my eyes and let out a heavy sigh, focusing intently on removing the shells from my boiled eggs.

She asked again, pleadingly, "Cassandra, tell me what he did to you."

The tone of her voice and the combination of those words bore into my heart. Suddenly, I couldn't see anything in front of me as my eyes filled with tears. I put down my half-peeled eggs, quickly washed my hands and went straight to my room, averting my eyes before she could see my tears. But it was too late. She followed me to my room, where I sat on my bed wiping the salty, unexpected tears. She wasn't being unkind, or being meddlesome; she genuinely wanted to know who had hurt her granddaughter. I wanted to tell her so badly.

She hugged me and said, "I'm sorry. I didn't want to make you cry. I won't bring it up again."

With that, I kept my silence.

6

I sat across from Teti, emphatically shaking my head. She had asked me if I wanted to tell somebody what had happened to me. No. I had sworn to myself that that I would take this secret to the grave. I remember thinking when I was younger that I wouldn't even be able to get away with that.

My mother had told me that when the world is over, Jesus Christ would come down from heaven with a large book and proceed to read aloud everyone's sins on Earth. So I thought, *not only am I going to Hell, but everyone is going to know what horrible things I did.*

After my uncle, my mom's only sibling, passed away when I was seven years old, my grandmother told me that he would be my guardian angel, explaining that he would be up in heaven watching over me and protecting me. At that age, I initially was comforted by the thought. I had just begun to fully grasp the concept of death and understood that I would never see my uncle alive again. I also understood that I would continue to hear the sobs of my grandmother through my bedroom wall into the night. So the thought of my loving uncle as my own personal angel and my own supernatural protection was the good that had come out of his death. I had my own personal body guard.

Nonetheless, the abuse continued, convincing me that my loving uncle had forsaken me. I imagined him peering through the clouds, with large beautiful wings, looking down at me, shaking his head at me and frowning in disapproval. In my shame-filled seven-year-old mind, I concluded that he had to have been disgusted by me and determined that he never did anything to help me. I remember at one point looking at one of those pins that people put on their car visors with the image of a guardian angel as a source of protection. I looked away; I no longer believed in guardian angels. In my world they didn't exist.

I was adamant about telling no one what happened to me. I felt fully responsible. I would also be fully responsible for ruining the family if I ever opened my mouth. I couldn't imagine what would happen if I were to ever tell the truth. Maybe no one would believe me. My mom may slap me across the face for telling alleged lies. My father could suggest that being in school for social work messed up my mind and that, in dealing with so many clients, I mistook their stories for my own. They could say that I've always had something against my father, and that's the reason I'm making up lies. My mother may be too scared to separate from him because she depends on him too much and may make a conscious decision that it's easier to not believe me.

Maybe everyone would believe me. And then what? The stress may affect my grandmother's heart and cause her to slip into a depression or, worse, cause a heart attack. My mom could become violent and assault my father, getting her in trouble with the law. My brother could become traumatized by his own father's actions and spiral out of control. Either way, nothing good could possibly come out of telling anyone. It was my problem, and nobody needed to know about it.

Part of the reason I could barely tolerate the intrusive thoughts or was barely able to speak aloud what my father did to me was the immense shame I felt. It wasn't just that I was afraid of what would happen to my family if I told; in exposing my father as a predator, I was also exposing my vile mark of Cain to the world. There was also my self-loathing, disgust, and guilt.

I had slept with my mother's husband, my own mother's husband. I was a home wrecker, and I would be punished for my actions. My karma was tarnished. I firmly believed that I could never possibly have a happy marriage. My husband would step out on me, and I would be cursed the way my mom seemed to be, and it was all my fault.

"It's not your fault," Teti would say.

My reply would be: "You're supposed to say that."

It was my fault and nothing she said would change that belief. I was dumb and gullible enough to be angry with my own mother. Not only did I partake in despicable activities, but I also had the nerve to be angry with my own mother for not fulfilling her duties as a wife. As my father had informed me, his sexual dissatisfaction with her was the reason he was coming to me. It had become my responsibility, and I had hated my mom for it.

Guilt was an understatement. When we would discuss child sexual abuse in class, they would talk about perpetrators using physical abuse or threats of violence. They would discuss how the perpetrator would threaten the child's family members. I didn't fit in any of those categories, which led me to the conclusion that I was a willing participant. I was fully responsible. Other kids like little Anya were able to come forward, but I was not. Why?

I would regularly watch *Law & Order: Special Victims Unit*, which frequently portrays child sexual abuse. Typically, there were threats or violence involved, furthering my isolation, and deepening my guilt. But on rare occasions, there would be a child who was sexually abused for years and who never said anything. As a matter of fact, they kept going back to the perpetrator, even cared for the perpetrator.

For one of the victims on the show, the predator had been his piano teacher who had given him his incredible piano talent. Despite the abuse, the boy idolized the man because he had taught him so much. For a different victim, it was his mentor and father-figure, who took him to baseball games, gave him beer, and showed him porn. Both of these children were confused as I was. They took the good despite the bad. The kids blamed themselves also for what happened. It was a very familiar story for me.

At one point, I became concerned over my father's wellbeing if I were to tell. Despite the sexual abuse that I endured, I had internalized the guilt and took so much responsibility for it that I did not want to hurt him. I thought: *He's getting old and his health is poor. Who will take care of him?* I would watch those episodes intently, asking, *Why? Why didn't those victims ever do anything?*

I brought these questions to Teti. It's hard to process and make sense of things that you did as a child when you consider yourself an intelligent, headstrong and independent adult. You don't want to consider yourself as ever being gullible, green, and easily malleable, but Teti helped me process things from a child's point of view. This was one of the most important conversations that I had with Teti. She helped me look at it as I would look at any child in my situation, as I would look at a client sitting across from me in therapy, telling me her story. She helped me take an objective perspective, separating the confusing emotions specific to my experience from the actual facts of the sexual abuse.

The sexual abuse takes place over eight years. It is evident that the adult, who is also the child's father, has authority over the five-year-old child. The child's mother is often absent, thus causing the father to become the dominant caregiver in the home. This is the foundation which the father uses to gradually become abusive towards the child. He initiates a grooming and indoctrination process, normalizing sexual behavior, gradually increasing the sexual activity over time. At the onset, the adult utilizes "privileges," such as staying up late to watch movies, and other forms of bribery, such as special attention and the title "daddy's girl." As the abuse progresses, the abuser influences the child's thought process, brainwashing her to believe and side with her primary caregiver and abuser. Furthermore, having been raised in a strict household, could the child really have objected to her father's requests? What would have been the consequences if the child did say no? Could it have led to physical abuse? After all, he was the sole disciplinarian in the home. The abuser had ensured that the family remained isolated. The child was not dealing with a stranger whom she could escape from.

Moreover, when one is sexually abused, there is the taboo subject of the visceral reactions that occur within the victim, causing him or her to think that he or she enjoys the abuse, furthering the guilt. The child does not realize that the same way that the body reacts to pain, it reacts to pleasure, something that is beyond his or her control. The extensive shame that occurs in the child who experiences any type of arousal may cause her to feel an inherently "bad," causing her to feel responsible for, or deserving of the violation. The child has also been raised in a culture in which family secrets, such as the adoption, are not openly discussed. What would be the potential legal repercussions of her revealing the truth? Maybe foster care, and worse, separation from her brother.

Had such a child come to me for help, I would never think to put blame on her. So why did I put blame on myself?

Ridding myself of guilt that I had carried for years was far easier said than done. I still had the immense shame to contend with. Even if it wasn't my fault, I still felt disgusted with myself, tainted. I wished it would go away, like a scar on one's body eventually fades and becomes forgotten. But this was different; the memories continued to haunt me. I couldn't shake the feeling of being filthy inside. I could never be un-touched.

7

I'm not exactly sure why the abuse ended. Maybe it was because he became much stricter with me as I became a teenager, causing him to be too wary to "ask" anymore. Or maybe I grew too old for his liking, causing him to stop and, as a result, have no reason to be nice to me. Either way, my father was the head of the household. Whatever he said went.

He had his own chair at the head of the table, which nobody else was ever allowed to sit in, ever. I passed off his strictness as the typical strictness of a Haitian patriarch, but as I got older and more attentive, I questioned his motives. Anything that could have a lock on it did, from the mailbox outside to his stereo system in the living room to my parents' bedroom. My mom, who was typically absent-minded with her belongings and had a carefree attitude about possession, went along with it. On numerous occasions she actually locked herself out of her own room. Even his work briefcase was locked, and not even my mother had any idea what the combination was.

My grandparents, who were the only ones in the home when my brother and I went to school during the day, took offense to the fact that everything was under lock-and-key; to them it suggested that they were viewed as crooks and thieves.

From what I observed, it was a suspicion of others, para-
noia, and something to hide. He identified himself as "overpro-
tective," but in actuality, he was controlling. He would open every piece of mail that came to the home, regardless of whether
or not it was addressed to him. Even if it were evidently junk
mail, he would open it just to make the point that it was *his*
mailbox and that he had the right to open anything that came
to *his* home. He would sometimes ban me from going out with
friends for no apparent reason at all. I never had a sleepover
because my friend's brother might have had "a secret agenda
for me at night." Ironic, isn't it? The more I strived towards independence as a teenager, the more it was twisted as me being
disrespectful, and my father tightened his grip on me further.

My father was idolized in my family. What a good man for
marrying my mom who already had a daughter, and adopting
her daughter to be his own. He was such a great husband for
allowing my mom's parents to stay at our home. He was a good
father for being strict and for being protective over me, protecting me from the dangers of the outside world.

When people came to visit, he often put on a show, giving
extra affection towards my Troy and me, with spontaneous
hugs, showing that he's "Dad." His voice was softer, and he used
terms such as "my boy" and "my darling daughter" when referring to my brother and I. He often engaged in discussions
where he gave his strong opinion about things that were moral-
ly right or wrong with family members. He expressed a certain
rigidity with rules and how things "must be." He read the Bible
every morning, although he only attended church once a year,
if at all.

He was portrayed as the perfect family man. He put on a good
performance, but the members of the household knew what the
reality was behind the scenes. My grandmother also questioned
his arrogance. When I was younger and he would check my
homework, he would insist on poking me forcefully in my forehead if there was something that I failed to understand, and my

grandmother swiftly corrected him in his method of so-called "discipline." She'd stick up for me and say that there were better ways of teaching, ones that did not involve putting me down. She was also insulted by the method in which he would "clean" the house. If the floor needed to be swept, he would sweep the trash into a pile on the floor and walk away, expecting someone else to pick it up, as if he was too good to stoop down and put it in a dustpan. But my grandmother kept quiet about that because after all, she was only a guest in his house.

Despite the feeling of being wronged by my parents, I constantly strived for their approval, for validation that I was a good daughter. I had walled off the memories of the abuse from other memories in my mind. It was like trying to keep it a secret from myself. The abuse never happened, and that violated girl no longer existed. Instead, I put all of my energy into being the successful girl who excelled academically and was liked by everyone. I was part of the National Honors Society, the Thespian Honors Society, earned top grades, and got a full scholarship to college—but if it wasn't perfect, it wasn't good enough. I was never good enough. I vied specifically for my mom's attention, for her to be proud of me, but it got to a point where doing well was expected of me and therefore went unnoticed.

I often resented the absence of Mom. It wasn't only because of her physical absence when she was working but also her lack of effort to make her own voice heard in the home. For instance, she never objected to my father's ludicrous decision that we must have dinner as a family in order to have family time but that dinner should be in complete silence because it was "rude" to talk at the table. To prevent reprimand by Father, hands had to be placed on the table, utensils could not audibly scrape the plates, and the only words allowed to be spoken were, "Could you please pass the dish?" This was short lived, however, as my brother and I quickly came up with ways to avoid being home for dinner by filling our schedules with extracurricular activities at school.

A more poignant incident occurred when Mom remained quiescent and close-mouthed when my father kicked me out of their bedroom. It had been about three weeks since I had spoken a word to him, nor he a word to me. The tension filled the air like a suffocating cologne. That day, while he was at work, I decided to sit on my mom's bed with her, as she watched a movie, attempting to build rapport and find some common ground with her.

When he came home from work, he entered his room, took one glance at me and abruptly said, "Get out of my room." The resentment in his voice was undeniable.

I looked at Mom, waiting for an objection. She gave no reaction. With that, I got up to leave.

As I got to the door, he said sternly, "No, sit down; you can stay." It was not a request. It was a demand, yet I proceeded to exit the room.

He then commanded, with even more authority in his voice, "Sit down!" He was asserting himself as dictator.

I hesitated in the doorway, looking to my mother again for a reaction, but there was none. Her face was expressionless, as she observed our interaction like a bystander. It was clear that my father had the final say, as I continued across the hall straight to my room.

"Where are you going?" he asked indignantly, clearly vexed by my decision to ignore his demand.

"I have homework to do," I shrugged. I wasn't surprised by his spitefully tyrannical reaction, but I felt abandoned by Mom. I was shocked that she did not so much as lift her pinky finger in my defense. It was as if she had given up her right to be my parent.

I wasn't alone in feeling this abandonment. I remember coming home from college to an argument between my father and brother about college. My brother had applied to various colleges and had been accepted to Rutgers, yet my father was angry because my brother had not received a scholarship. It

was only a few days before the deadline to make the initial payment for Troy's freshman year, and Father was refusing to pay.
Instead, he took it as an opportunity to harass Troy about how
he could've done better academically, or athletically, or that
he should've applied to more scholarship programs so that he
could've gotten a scholarship. Father was clearly using the power that he knew he had over Troy, making threats that Troy may
not go to college at all.

Over the years, as Troy grew from a young boy to a young
man, Father could no longer use physical intimidation towards him, so he resorted to financial means of intimidation
and harassment. When Troy eventually had the funds to purchase his own items, such as video games or gym equipment,
the bitterness from Father was evident, and Troy would never
hear the end of his "reckless" spending habits. On one occasion, Father forced Troy to put his gym equipment outside, on
the back porch where it would inevitably rust, because there
was "no room" for such items in the spare room, which nobody
occupied.

Troy's huge life-changing decision to go to college was
Father's ideal opportunity to rub in Troy's face that he, Pierre
Baptiste, was in charge of Troy's life. Lifelong discussions of
having a college fund were suddenly nugatory. Since birth, Troy
and I were told that there were funds put aside for our college
education, but when it came time for college tuition to be paid,
the money had mysteriously vanished. Now, my brother stood
in the dining room, getting viciously reprimanded by Pierre for
inadequate preparation, his future uncertain. Again, Mother
watched from the sidelines and remained mum throughout the
discussion. Eventually, it was I was I who came to my brother's defense, pointing out that further discussion on what could
have been done was futile and stressing the importance of
Troy's academic future at Rutgers.

Even my grandparents felt abandoned by their daughter.
My grandfather had worked for years in the country in a fish

factory to earn money for his family. He often recounted stories of enduring bitter winters in Brooklyn, New York, rising early to wait for the bus "when it was so cold that if you spit, it would turn to ice before it hit the ground." He then spent hours working at Marshall's, a factory where he was surrounded by the stench of fish and endless ice. As a man who was habituated to a consistent 90-degree tropical weather, this was misery. He eventually retired and was able to enjoy time in his home country. Since he had a bank account in the United States, and often flew back to Haiti, he gave my parents access to his account in order for them to send him money in Haiti when needed. Unfortunately, my grandfather put all of his trust in Pierre— my mother barely monitored her own account, let alone my grandfather's. So Pierre was solely responsible for depositing Grandfather's social security check when it arrived in the mail and for withdrawing money when it needed to be sent to Haiti.

After over a decade of Pierre managing Grandpa's funds, Grandpa finally asked to see his bank account. It was a great shock when Grandpa noticed that he only had a few thousand dollars to his name. He had handed over his account with over fifteen thousand dollars in it. The biggest question that continues to haunt my grandpa to this day is "where did the money go?" Sadly, this was also a time period when Grandpa started to be affected by mild dementia.

Pierre had no explanations of where the money went, but Grandma remembered certain odd statements from Pierre throughout the years. When she had asked Pierre to tell Grandpa how much he had in his account, he replied, "For what? So he can waste all of it?" He also had admitted to borrowing some of Grandpa's money so that he could "start a business." The doubts and uncertainty led to distrust and seemed to make Grandpa's symptoms even worse, causing him to stay up at night reciting stories about how hard he worked and how much money was in his account. He felt swindled, cheated, and was not shy about voicing his concerns. Conflict arose around

Pierre's role in my grandfather's agitation, causing additional tension in the house. Despite the conflict, Mother's presence was nowhere to be found. She did not search for a solution to the problem, she did not attempt to calm Grandpa's nerves, and she did not intervene and take responsibility for the account. She remained absent, leaving my grandparents—her parents—dismayed at her inaction.

I soon determined that there were two people in my family that I would put my energy into, and they were my brother and grandmother. I stopped trying to be the unachievable "perfect child." I would laugh to myself when my mother would say things like, "Friends come and go, but family will always be there." My experience had taught me that that wasn't the case. I gave up on the idea that my parents could ever be the supportive, loving, and available parents seen on TV or in my friends' homes.

At the age of nineteen, I had built up much resentment and infuriation towards my parents. It was my first summer break from college. I had returned home, after two semesters away, hoping things might have improved, but I was wrong. The way I was being treated, I felt like an indentured servant. As the "young lady of the house," I was the dishwasher, the duster, the cleaner, and the organizer. I remember learning that, according to Haitian culture, a girl is not considered a woman until she is married with children. It was the transition from the property of the father to the property of her husband. I was absolutely floored at the antiquated and chauvinistic philosophy my parents still held on to in the twenty-first century. As an individual residing in America, I considered myself an accomplished, independent and intelligent young woman, but at home I was nothing more than a little girl.

Since my mother wasn't one who would even consider entertaining a conversation with me about my woes, I wrote a long letter to my father, to persuade him to understand how oppressive he was being. I explained how I felt hurt for him not trusting me, as I had given my parents no reason whatsoever to mistrust me. I was a good student. I strived to be perfect for my parents. I was obedient. Nonetheless, I felt that I was in a state of continuous punishment for not doing anything wrong at all. The way I lived my life was the way others my age experienced being grounded. I wasn't allowed to go out, I wasn't allowed to borrow the car, and I felt like a prisoner. It was worse than being treated like a child; I was being treated like a delinquent. Friends advised me to simply do what I wanted anyway, "teach them a lesson," but I could not bring myself to cause conflict or be seen as disrespectful.

I outlined in the letter how it was unfair for him to open my mail, because he should respect my privacy. His excuse was that he wanted to keep me "safe" but I didn't see how opening my bank statements was a means of keeping me safe; rather, it was means to intrude on my privacy and maintain control over me. I wrote about how other parents who have kids who are "bad" let them do much more than I was allowed to. I wrote that other kids were into drugs, were sneaking out, and cursed at their parents, among countless other things. I expressed frustration that at home, I was seen as an evil person, but at school, work, and other people's homes, people appreciated me and respected me for who I was. I also briefly mentioned that my father was wrong for violating me in the way that he did. I didn't feel that the letter was complete without that part. I had deleted it and re-written it many times until I was satisfied.

I delivered the completed letter to his room in an envelope with his name on it. It came out to be four pages long. I felt a complex mixture of emotions. I felt justified in expressing my thoughts and feelings as a young adult. By approaching my father in an articulate and logical manner, I felt that he had no choice but to accept that. At the same token, it was something I had never done before. I feared his reaction to my bluntness. Yet, I had nothing to lose. I was already living like a prisoner; I couldn't imagine that things could get much worse. As it turned out, I was naïve to think that I could reason with my oppressive father.

My father read the letter and did not speak a word to me for days. He did not utter one word in my direction. The wait was nerve-wrecking. On the day he finally decided to speak to me, he asked that I meet with him downstairs, in the den. He had the letter in his hand, and sat for a moment in silence, while he tried to formulate his words. His hand was balled into a fist, and he was breathing heavily, exasperated.

When he finally spoke, it was through his teeth, "I think about what happened and it hurts me every day; how dare you bring that up to me! Don't you ever mention it again." He was referring to the years of sexual abuse that I mentioned in my letter.

I was stunned into silence. I was perplexed by his egocentric approach on the matter, and for a second I actually questioned me being inconsiderate of his feelings. He knew that he had wronged me, but blamed me for reminding him of the pain *he* endured.

Before I could reply, he continued, "Mail comes to my house. So I have a right to open it. If you think otherwise, you can afford a P.O. Box." He went on to obliterate my letter, one point after another, without letting me get a word edgewise. I was absolutely speechless. At the age of nineteen, I felt no different than I did when he told me what to do at the age of six.

Right after graduation from undergraduate school, I decided to run my own business, far away from home, so that I could have enough income to pay for graduate school and get my own place. It was my opportunity to become independent. I had been working as a sales representative for almost two years selling fine cutlery, just to pay my bills while at school, and I got promoted to district manager. I excitedly designed a business plan, searched for an office space, signed a lease, and went head first into running my very own business.

Initially, it was slow as expected, as I focused all of my energy on advertisement and recruiting to fill positions. I didn't have the funds to run a business *and* get an apartment, so I was willing to make the necessary sacrifices and sleep in my office. Instead of an apartment, I got a cheap gym membership. I woke up early every morning, did a 20 minute exercise, took a shower, and got ready for my day. I worked twelve-hour days, from sun up until sundown, building from scratch. I worked hard, was dedicated to my work, and was motivated to be successful on my own. Summer hit and my office was suddenly full of college students, eager to make some cash, and add experience to their resumes.

Business was great...for five months. It was probably the worst time to run a business as the economy took a nosedive in 2008. When summer ended, my salespeople vanished to out-of-town colleges. As amazing as the product was, it could not be sold effectively in stores, required face-to-face in-home demonstrations, something many older adults were not interested in doing. My office was soon as empty as my bank account. When my diet consisted of carrots and peanut butter sandwiches, I decided it was time to close my doors, and regretfully packed my things to go back home. I had graduated at the peak of the recession, resulting in numerous layoffs for existing employees and very few jobs for recent graduates—namely me. Again, I had to be dependent on my parents.

Frustration mounted as I felt absolutely trapped, with not enough financial freedom to move out. I tried to become as independent of my parents as possible, while under their roof. As soon as I got a stable job, I put in hours upon hours of overtime in order to purchase a car. This was my first successful step towards independence. There would be no threats of taking it away if I were too "disobedient." After I bought a car, I kept a lookout for affordable apartments. Unfortunately, with the car payment and insurance payments, I could not find an affordable apartment in my area near my workplace; not even a studio apartment would enable me to eat more than canned beans based on my entry-level income.

Countless times, I vowed to get out of my house. I could not tolerate the thought of being trapped despite my efforts to become successfully independent. My tiny bedroom became my sacred abode. It barely contained my bed, my TV and two small nightstands. But it was *my* space; it was where I spent almost all of my time. I was a house mouse, creeping out only when I needed food or drink. When I did occasionally encounter my father, I realized that I had to pick and choose my battles. Do I get a birthday card to keep the peace, or do I not say a word at all? Do I smile and say good morning, or do I give him the cold shoulder? Pierre didn't like my independent thinking, and frequently mentioned how much he regretted "sending me" to stay on campus at college. I had developed too much of a backbone for his liking.

8

eti never pushed me into disclosing my abuse. Although I was very set in my decision to take my secret to the grave, it was something that I still struggled with internally. I wrote in my journal:

I went to Ash Wednesday mass today and the theme was repentance for our sins. I thought hard about that theme and how I'm striving to become a better person mentally, physically and spiritually. In church, I repeated to myself one line of the Our Father: "Forgive us our trespasses, as we forgive those who trespass against us." I felt good coming to church and working on my sins, but I felt bad because I questioned myself, "Have I, or can I forgive him? And what is forgiveness?" Does God want me to forgive him in my heart and continue having him as a part of my life? Or can forgiveness be me forgiving him in my heart, but still exposing him for what he did to me? And if or when I do so, should I be mad if my mom forgives him? I really don't know. This makes me think of the tons of priests that molested the young boys in the church—would

*God have liked the boys to remain silent, or better, re-
move the so-called servants of God from the church for
their despicable actions? Jesus forgave Judas, Mary
Magdalene, and even those who killed him. But it was
his destiny to die on the cross. Is it my destiny to suffer
in silence?*

I wanted very much to do the right thing. I didn't want to
tell so that I could protect my family from heartache. I imagined that opening my mouth would cause an explosion of fury,
blowing the roof off of my house. People would be intensely
astonished, heartbroken and infuriated with me. I debated,
*would one rather know that one is lying with a monster, and
live with heartache, or would one rather not know, and continue living in ignorant bliss?*

As I worked with Teti, I started thinking more about the repercussions of not divulging my secret and the impact it may
have on others. My father's brother had two beautiful and energetic girls with his wife: Krystall and Jacqueline. I was in love
with them. The eldest, Krystall, was four years old and like a little
grown-up. She was Miss Independent, running around, wanting
to be involved with the adults. Her baby sister, Jacqueline, who
was two years old, was trying to keep up with her much quicker
and older sister in her awkward and wobbly run.

I had seriously bonded with Krystall, and volunteered to
take care of her, when she had come home from the hospital
after being born. I remember my very first night with her: she
had fallen asleep, and I spent hours watching her. Since she was
born premature, she had gotten a cold, and her breathing was
rattled due to the congestion in her nostrils. I must've stayed
up just watching her until about two in the morning, until I
was too exhausted and started to drift off to sleep. Of course,
little Krystall took that as her cue to wake up. I didn't get any
sleep that night, but I continued to volunteer to babysit my little
buddy. It was amazing to watch her learn to crawl, walk, speak

and explore the world. It was also fun to watch her interact with her new little sister and change roles from the baby to the older sister. Both girls seemed to have sprouted every time they would visit.

One day, the whole family came by to visit. It was a Sunday, and they came right after church. The girls were absolutely full of energy and were running around in their beautiful church dresses and nicely braided hair. My brother and I were playing with the girls while paying attention to a Jenga game, which we were playing with my uncle.

I had the youngest, Jacqueline, on my lap with my left arm around her and played Jenga with my free right hand. This was my uncle's first time playing the game, and he was boasting loudly about his skills. Troy teased him playfully, yet competitively. Mother was in the kitchen, preparing the Sunday meal. There was laughter between her and my uncle's wife, as they gossiped about co-workers. In between taking turns for the game, Troy and I intermittently played with the girls, but the girls wanted in on the action.

Krystall was walking around the table from one person to the next asking if she could play. She was not satisfied with recommendations to play with other toys; she wanted to play with the grown-ups and kept reaching for the blocks. Of course, in an intense game of Jenga, that was a no-no, and she was shooed away. Feeling rejected, Krystall sulked and pouted as she walked away. Pierre happened to be down the hallway, where he was going into his room, around the corner. He saw her frown and said, "What's wrong honey?" Looking for attention and consolation, Krystall followed my father into the hallway, completely out of my sight.

I immediately felt intensely overwhelmed with panic. My heart fluttered like the wings of a butterfly in the presence of a cat. My attention was torn completely away from the game. I called out her name as calmly as I could, making a conscious effort to rid my voice of the panic I felt inside. She quickly came back to me and stayed in the common area. The wrenching of my gut began to ease, but I stayed on guard. From then on, I would always tend to the girls when they visited and keep them busy with my brother or me. If they wanted to sit on someone's lap, I made sure it was mine and not my father's. Before these beautiful girls, I only had myself to worry about. After that initial feeling of panic, I became concerned for their safety, as well for the safety of my future children.

9

While I was working with Teti, I was also falling in love. I had started a long-distance relationship with Micah, my best male friend from college. We had continued to keep in touch with each other even after he moved to be with his family in Georgia after graduation. We had kept each other abreast on current happenings, from him shaving his head bald to me becoming a red-head. After ending a relationship that I had no business being in to begin with, I followed Teti's advice on correcting my divining rod.

The guy I had been involved with had red flags and alarm bells going off in my head. He was the type of guy who enjoyed "that's what she said" jokes and farting games. I should've gracefully exited when he informed me that he didn't "believe in therapy," as if what I was spending thousands of dollars on in schooling and doing for a living did not exist. Needless to say, he was not a good match. But he was a nice and caring guy. Knowing full well that this wasn't the guy for me, I settled for having *someone* rather than be with no one at all. Teti had been right; I knew exactly what I wanted but continuously settled, bypassing all warning signs and red flags.

I made the decision that I was no longer going to settle, and if that meant being single, then so be it. I was too busy with school, work, and my internship to be in a relationship anyway, so why look for it? I was disheartened and I was genuinely giving up. I thought I did everything I was *supposed* to do; I had been a great student in high school, was taking college courses, and was involved in numerous extracurricular activities. I had anticipated falling in love with my future husband in college, and then getting married after graduation. To my dismay, life did not unfold as my dreams did. I figured: Well, then I will surely find my love in graduate school. But to my surprise, most of my classmates were female, and the few males I encountered were gay—just my luck. I knew that I was a fit, attractive, and intelligent young woman, but I had no luck in finding my prince charming. I felt that the only explanation was madichon, my curse and my karma coming into play. Either way, at least I had the power to do myself justice by following my gut and refusing to settle for people who would inevitably lead to heartbreak, and I was firm in that decision.

I believe that it was fate that brought me to Micah. During a time in which I thought it would've been the worst idea to enter a relationship, God granted me the clarity to see that Micah possessed all of the qualities that I looked for in a life partner. I had been nonchalantly rambling to my co-worker Cara about my close friendship with Micah and shared how much I adored him. He was a great listener, easy to talk to, and made me feel so good with his love and support. As a matter of fact, I felt quite comfortable telling him that I loved him, and he said the same to me. While talking to Cara, I caught myself mid-sentence and realized, *Dear God, Micah is my perfect match.* But I had never seen him in a romantic light before. I tried to brush it off as the caring love for a friend, but the conversation clearly shifted as I asked Cara, "Have you ever dated a friend before?"

The frequency of communication between Micah and I increased. I was curious to explore what was there. As we often did, we discussed our poor luck with the opposite sex in relationships. I told him about my vow to take a break from relationships to avoid settling for less than I deserved. He agreed with my decision. When we were in college, he had never approved of my previous relationships with men, and was proud of my choice.

We started talking every day, all day; while at work, we would text incessantly, and at night, we would talk until we fell asleep on the phone. I was amazed that after six years of friendship, we were able to speak to each other with a new-found enthusiasm and excitement for hours and hours. As matter of fact, when we had first met each other in college, it was no different; we would talk on the phone for three hours at a time. I remember our first phone conversation, when we shared and laughed about childhood memories, learned that our favorite movie was *Jurassic Park,* and shared surprising details about ourselves—never getting bored. Years later, the ease of conversation was no different, but this time, I was viewing him through completely different lenses, in a much clearer light.

One day, while cleaning my room, I came across a half-finished scrap book that I started in college. I smiled at all of the crazy pictures we had taken of one another, from lounging to partying. Then I came across a page labeled, "Ideal Man." On small colored pieces of paper, my roommates and I had written all of the traits that we saw in our future husbands. I read the adjectives scrawled in my handwriting on the piece of green paper: *Tall, dark-skinned/tan, funny, sensitive, confident, profound, cultured, articulate, nice smile, family-oriented, open-minded...* The list was long, and to my disbelief, Micah met every single criteria but two. He didn't speak a different language, and he didn't have a six-pack, but those things, I could live without. The universe was certainly sending me some strong signals.

I was fearful of telling Micah about my romantic feelings towards him; I didn't want to make things awkward so instead made a joke during one of our late-night text conversations.

I sat on my bed, and I pecked, "We should just get married, since we can't seem to find ourselves a partner, LOL." I hit send and held my breath, wondering if he would pass this classic "Cassandra test."

He replied, "I'm serious when I say I want to marry you, no more 'LOL's' attached."

I squinted at my phone, rereading the text on its screen. I suddenly felt light-headed, as my body tingled with the thrill from an amusement park free fall. I focused my eyes and confirmed that they had not deceived me. What I thought I read was in fact present, in black and white. I felt the corners of my mouth lift into an irrepressible grin; the dimples in my cheeks started to burn. My phone chimed again.

"I've known that since freshman year," he continued.

I was flabbergasted, my mind totally blown. I fell back onto my bed, rolled onto my stomach, and then texted back, "You're lying."

"Call me," was his response.

I burst into my brother's room, like a giddy five-year-old, skipping and grinning, talking a mile-a-minute about what had happened. "Call him," my brother said matter-of-factly, barely removing his eyes from the video game on his TV screen.

I returned back to my room, scrolled through "Recent Calls" and pressed "Send" on Micah's picture. My heart was drumming as the phone rang, and I waited for him to pick up.

What ensued was an amazing eye-opening phone conversation that lasted until the early hours of the morning. He revealed to me that he had been interested in a romantic relationship with me since our very first three-hour-long phone call. I wondered why he wasn't more aggressive in his pursuit.

He said that he valued our friendship, too much to consider pushing me towards a relationship I wasn't ready for. He wanted to appreciate me fully for the person I am, not just my physical representation. I did sense that there was a possibility that Micah had romantic feelings towards me freshman year, but dismissed them and paid attention to our budding friendship. Yet who would think that such feelings would last years later? I bust his chops for not being successful at getting me sooner, but I know that I hadn't been ready for Micah in my college years.

Micah had said to me once before, "Sometimes, people are brought into your life so that you know exactly what you don't want in your life." I needed to go through the disappointment of settling for less before I realized that I truly deserved more. With Micah, I allowed myself to love and to be loved. It was a strange yet exhilarating feeling to be able to put a face on the prince charming that all little girls dream about. I had never felt such strong emotions before. My heart was playing hopscotch, butterflies made a permanent residence in my stomach, and I had the feeling that I was floating. I joked that I should either check myself into a hospital or a mental health clinic based on my symptoms.

In a time in which I was overwhelmed with a seven-day week, involving forty hours of work, twenty-one hours of internship, and a full Saturday of classes, God granted us the ability to engage in a relationship in which we could explore the depths of one another's being and achieve intimacy through the only tool we had: communication. My faith was renewed, and my curse had been lifted. There was no room in my schedule for dating, going to the movies, and having dinners. I knew that this relationship was not a decision, nor was it a result of my actions; it was destined.

Micah had waited years for me, and despite a move 800 miles away, and after many girlfriends, his heart stubbornly remained for me alone. It was fate that brought Micah and I together, and at the perfect time. We spoke on the telephone for hours, and expounded on topics that other couples probably wouldn't have begun to explore until much later in a typical relationship. We discussed beliefs on disciplining children, experiencing grief, money management, and a medley other topics.

Micah was also subjected to incessant "Cassandra Tests." They ranged from reasonable, "What would you do if I survived a horrible accident and was disfigured," to outlandish, "What would you do if I told you that I was once a male?" Micah passed every single test with flying colors, no matter how hard I tried. Our compatibility was undeniable. The trust that we had in each other was already present through our friendship, making it much easier for me to accept to his love. My guard was down, heart open, and access granted. It was easy to love Micah; I had already loved him as a friend. But to allow myself to *be* loved produces the most extraordinary, inimitable, and liberating feeling that is a blessing to experience. It wasn't long until I started thinking about my future with him: married, in love, and with children.

I had previously been willing to keep my mouth shut, to prevent grief from my family, but I started to think about the family that I planned to have one day. Ever since I was a little girl, I thought about having a completely different type of family than the one I grew up in. In observing my parents, I would make a mental note, "Don't be like them when you have kids." I imagined a loving and warm home. One in which I had open communication with my children. One in which I knew who my children were, as individuals, acknowledging and respecting their different personalities. One in which my husband and I would be loving towards one another, and equally involved in the decision-making for our children. I would always have an open-door policy with my kids, and they would know that they could come to me or my husband for anything. I imagined myself as a supportive parent, going to recitals, plays, meets, matches, and games. We would have dinner together, excitedly sharing the happenings of our day. I saw vibrant, enthusiastic, loving, intelligent and talented children. I saw siblings treating one another like the best of friends, despite occasional quarrels. I envisioned a home filled with laughter, I dreamt of a beautiful and tightly-knit family.

Then I thought: *Well what about my kids' relationship with their grandparents?* I could see my mom spoiling my kids, purchasing clothes, and toys for them, volunteering to babysit on a date-night, teaching me how to warm the bottle to feed them, and giving me lessons on Haitian superstitions when it came to babies. Her eyes often lit up with babies, and I was sure that she would be proud to be a grandparent.

Then my thoughts shifted to my father holding my bundle of joy in his hands. The mere thought of him touching my baby was unnerving. I couldn't stomach the thought. It was as if his evilness would seep through the baby's blanket and clothes, and poison my precious child. I couldn't let that happen. After the incident with Krystall, I didn't think I would be able to contain my reaction.

I envisioned my wedding day. I saw myself in a beautiful white gown, nervously holding my bouquet of flowers as I walked down the aisle to marry the love of my life. Could I have Pierre, him with his arm through mine, walk me down the aisle to give me away to my future husband? I didn't think I could do it. The vows exchanged between my husband and me on the day of our wedding, in a church, in front of God, would be sacred. It would be a profession of the profound love and respect that we have for one another. The mere presence of my father at the ceremony—a man who not only disregarded his own wedding vows, but also violated my rights as a child—would be blasphemous and intolerable. I would rather walk down the aisle alone before I could consider giving my father the honor of giving me away at my wedding. I couldn't do it. I just couldn't.

I found myself in a completely different mental space. What was I to do? What excuse could I give as to why I didn't want Pierre breathing the same air as my children? How could I explain to my mom and the rest of my family that I didn't want my father to walk me down the aisle without being criticized or badmouthed for breaking tradition?

10

fter much thought, I realized that I was tired. I was tired of making excuses. By holding in this secret, my father stayed safe in his roles as the victim and the dictator, whereas I was seen as the unreasonably angry and ungrateful daughter. I realized that the line had to be drawn somewhere. I always thought that I had to endure the sexual abuse because I had no other place to call home. I told myself that I would take this secret to the grave because once I was grown and moved out, it would no longer any impact on my life; I would no longer be under my parent's rule.

That was not the case. My cousins were in potential danger. Never before had I considered that my future children would be placed in potential danger by harboring this secret. I didn't give it a second thought when it came to sacrificing my happiness to keep the peace. But the thought of other children—my children—being put in harm's way, simply to shield a man from being exposed for what he was, was not an option. I refused to let the cycle of unprotected children continue. If it started with me, then it was to end with me.

I had to find a way to protect others. I made the life-changing decision that I could not move forward without disclosing what happened to me. I was ready to live freely and put this secret behind me for good. In search of further inspiration, I came across this quote by Ambrose Redmoon: "Courage is not the absence of fear; rather, it's the judgment that something else is more important than fear." I was terrified about the choice I had made, but I had to be courageous—my future depended on it.

Once I made the decision to tell, I became completely engrossed in planning different ways of disclosure. Who would I tell? How would I tell? When would I tell? Where would I tell? I became more avid in hunting for apartments, because I had to ensure my safety out of the house before I would utter a word of my disclosure.

I had visions of inviting my mother to my new apartment. That way I'd be in my own place, and safe. Maybe I'd tell her over drinks. I thought perhaps the alcohol would relieve the tension, or worse, raise it. But would my mother even drive to my apartment alone? She never came to visit me on campus on her own. I'd probably have to drive her. But what if our conversation ended with a blow-up? I couldn't imagine riding in a car with her after that. It's not like I had the money to get my own apartment anyway, so that plan went out the window before it even hatched.

I thought of telling my grandmother, because I knew without a shadow of a doubt that she would believe me. But when could I tell her? She was only in the states for a few months at a time, and I didn't want to tell her over the phone. And if she were in Haiti, I would have to fly over fifteen-hundred miles to tell her, but at least I would be safely out of the country, away from my mom when my grandmother told my mom over the phone. Yet, that plan became far too complicated. It made more sense to tell my mom directly.

At the same time, Micah and I were discussing whether he should move to New Jersey from Georgia or if I should move to Georgia from New Jersey. We had been in a long-distance relationship for over a year, and it was time to take our relationship to the next level, so something had to give and somebody had to make a move.

We debated and made extensive pros and cons lists. He was established with his job and his own apartment. Furthermore, Georgia's much lower real-estate prices allowed me to rent twice the amount of space that Jersey would offer, with half the amount of money. Ultimately, we decided that I would make the move to Georgia after graduating with my master's degree. Wanting to avoid a direct confrontation with my mom, my plan changed from verbal disclosure to the safer option of writing her a letter. First, I thought I would give it to her right before I moved to Georgia. Or just in case I didn't want to be around for the blow-up, I would leave the letter in a conspicuous location—maybe under her mattress—pray that Pierre did not find it before her, and direct her to find it and read it after I was already moved out of the house. I must've gone through at least thirty different scenarios, and it became increasingly apparent that I could not satisfy my avoidant-nature, and I had no choice but to come up with a way to face this head-on, and face-to-face.

This decision was followed by an intense smorgasbord of emotions: excitement, fear, anxiety, apprehension, everything all at once. Teti encouraged me to move beyond the logistics of telling and to focus on my feelings related to my resolution to finally reveal my sexual abuse after so many years. But at that moment, my feelings were secondary; I didn't like having uncertainty in my future, and my deepest fear was not knowing how my mother would react to the news. I needed to plan. I needed to know.

I started looking for evidence in everyday things for a glimpse of what my future would hold. I saw symbolism in everything. For instance, there were times that Mom would give me an extra-long, penetrating gaze, as if she were trying to read my mind. I would become panicked, convinced that she knew what I was plotting.

On one occasion, for the first time in my 24 years of knowing her, my mom had too much to drink. She was never a drinker to begin with; she would rarely have some Manichewitz wine—which is like grape juice—on holidays, such as Christmas and Thanksgiving. But on this particular day, we were having a barbeque, she wanted to try some wine coolers, and my uncle had brought over some liquor. I'm not sure how much she had, but she quickly appeared giddy, laughing and making jokes. She had the tendency of slapping the table when she laughed, even when she was sober. It had become more prevalent now that she was drunk, growing from the clap of a flyswatter to the wallop of a hammer.

I happened to be sitting next to her when, out of nowhere, she reached out, grabbed my ponytail, and pulled on it with full force. My head jolted back, and I suppressed my natural instinct to retaliate. I grabbed her firmly by the wrist and stared hard at her for a few seconds before I let go. I judged that it would be best that I excuse myself and return to my room. As I stood up, she attempted to lunge at me once more, giggling. Numerous thoughts swirled in my head. What would drive her to do that? Did I do something to trigger such a response? Did she want me to feel pain? Was this just a joke? Or were her inhibitions down, revealing her true feelings for me? They say that a drunken man tells no tales. She did not explicitly say anything to me, but her actions were loud and clear.

There must have been some dislike for me already existing inside her. Maybe that's an understatement; people don't attack other people out of *dislike*. She definitely had some serious animosity towards me. I remembered the scene in the movie *Precious* in which Precious's mother tearfully expresses that her sexually-abused daughter had stolen her man and that ever since she was born, her man would dismiss her, and reach instead for her daughter, Precious. She hated Precious for that.

On another occasion, my darling mother called me a bitch. The reason? I couldn't find a particular ingredient at the grocery store, so instead I got a substitute. She said that I was an idiot and that I was worthless. It was not uncommon for my mom to be condescending to me; she would occasionally call me a *jeness*, or slut, for wearing sexy clothes or because I chose to use tampons, or tell me I couldn't find a man because I couldn't cook to her liking. Sadly, most of the words she spoke to me were criticizing and demeaning. Typically I never provided a response, but her harsh words in reaction to something as trivial as an ingredient on her grocery list were unwarranted and hurtful.

I put the last grocery item into the fridge and shut the door. I turned around to face her, where she stood on the opposite side of the kitchen. I observed her face, which was unperturbed by the insults that had just left her mouth. She hadn't given it a second thought.

I shrugged, "I guess I learn from the best," as I balled up the plastic grocery bags in my hands. It was a reminder that I was her daughter, that by insulting me, she was insulting herself.

In truth, she had never had the patience to teach me to cook, volunteer to go shopping with me, teach me about make-up, or do the things that TV moms did. If I was unable to do things, it was due to her lack of teaching.

I think some part of her knew that, too. She glared at me for my response and said in her thick Haitian accent, "You are a bitch. You are a big-mouth bitch."

I stood in the kitchen, stunned to silence.

A few days later, I told my mother that she was not to attend my graduation. "How could you tell your own mother not to go to your graduation?" she asked, appalled. I pointed out that she had called me a bitch only a few days prior, wondering why she wanted to go in the first place. She responded, "You were acting like a bitch!" It didn't take too long for Pierre to get involved, stating that there should be better communication in the home, stating "we're family" and other bullshit.

I was out by the pool when I received a text message from my mother that read, "I'm sorry about what I said. It was an accident. I love you." It was clear that this was keyed by my father, as my mother had never been a savvy texter to provide accurate spelling, complete with punctuation and proper grammar. Despite all of this, I held on firmly on to fantasy that the loving and nurturing mom I once knew was still there, somewhere inside her. I was on the fence about her and how she would react to me. I could not wholly convince myself that she would support me, yet I could not lead myself to believe that she could whole-heartedly reject me either.

Although my mother professed to be an independent woman, there was a large gap between her perception of herself and reality. She talked about having the final say about decisions made in the home and doing whatever she wanted to do. In all honesty, she was highly dependent on my father. All cars were in his name. My mother didn't own credit cards, but my father did. So if she ever needed to order something from online or the television, she had to ask permission for his credit card. Pierre was responsible for writing checks and paying the bills in the house. She worked less than five minutes from the house, and would only drive to places in close proximity to the home. If she was ever required to go somewhere that was unfamiliar to her, my father was responsible for taking her. She may have believed that she ran things, but in actuality, on paper, it was he who ran her life. This was an important factor in how she would react to my disclosure, which caused me to have very little faith that she would even *want* to believe me. Essentially, she would have to choose between her daughter and her husband.

In one journal entry, I wrote:

Who takes precedence? Your parents, your marriage, or your children? Chronologically, you've known your

*parents all of your life—they cared for you and nur-
tured you from birth. There's love and respect. Then
there's your spouse, a person you chose to love and
spend the rest of your life with. Then there are your
children, born of your body, who you watched grow
and to whom you give unconditional love. What happens when you have to choose between these people?
I can't imagine having to choose. Some people have
said, "Put your marriage above all else; children will
grow up and move away and parents won't always be
around." Others would argue that children come before anyone and anything, regardless of the situation.
I wonder what Mom's philosophy is.*

My brother and I were never very affectionate to my mother, nor was she towards us. There was never a real affectionate
vibe in my house growing up anyway. We weren't the TV family who exchanged "I love you's" and gave hugs for "a job well
done." As parents, they felt that their own role was to discipline and prepare my brother and me for the world, so that we
could eventually care for them in old age. A parent's role was
not to care about your emotions, or to provide a shoulder to cry
on. Instead it was to "train" you to be a successful adult. As a
matter of fact, being a successful adult had nothing to do with
happiness.

If there were problems between my mom and brother or
between my mom and me, my father was the only one who
mediated. She went through a period of two years when she
was utterly intolerable. Her menopausal mood-swings were
unpredictable and dramatic. She acted like a toddler, having tantrums, craving attention. Troy and I would ignore her
banshee-like screams. My father, on the other hand, would do
whatever was necessary to appease her. He was willing to walk
on eggshells for her. He seemed to have endless patience for her,
while my brother and I did not. Also, my mother was fifty-five

years old and was not in the best health. She had recently found out that she was diabetic in addition to her previous diagnoses of high blood pressure and high cholesterol. Moreover, she had been married for over twenty years to a man who was suffering from loss of eyesight due to many years of glaucoma. I didn't think that I stood a chance, against my mom's extreme dependence on my father, or, for that matter, his dependence on her.

Conversely, there were times that I felt that I had a glimmer of hope. In typical fashion, I conducted Cassandra tests with her. Test number one: One afternoon, I convinced her to change the channel and watch Oprah. She loved Oprah. This particular episode was about men who had been sexually abused by their mothers. It wasn't my exact story but it was close enough. When I asked her later about it, she said she only watched a few minutes of it because it made her sick. She said, "I don't know what I would do if someone did that to my child. I would make them pay. Ooooh I would..." She couldn't finish her sentence. It was as if putting her thoughts into words would cause collateral damage. Test number two: I told my mom that I had a client who got married recently and seemed to be picking her husband over her son. She was appalled. She replied, "That's a shame, to pick a man over your own child." I was pleased with this response. Maybe there was hope after all.

I truly struggled with my thoughts about Mom; I was completely uncertain about her. There were so many conflicting factors to consider, from our existing relationship with one another, her role as a mother, her loving nature when I was a child, to whether she was to be blamed for my lack of protection as a child.

I clearly remember walking with my mom from my elementary school while we still lived in Philadelphia. I was full of energy, as I rattled on about what I did and learned at school that day. She held my left hand as we got ready to cross the big boulevard before the street my house was on. While we waited for the light to turn, she looked down at me and sternly said, "You know, moms know everything."

"Everything?" I asked.

She looked down at me with a very serious expression on her face and said, "We know everything."

I was both amazed and terrified at this sudden understanding. At the age of seven, I was convinced that my mom had super powers. I wondered if she could look at me and read my mind with a special x-ray vision. Or maybe every time she touched me, information would be transferred straight to her. What if all mothers just have a connection with their daughters forever, and even if I were to do something bad at school, she would know instantly even if she were all the way at work? For a whole week, I was on my utmost best behavior. As a seven year old, I could only be on my best behavior for so long, but my mother's words were certainly etched in my mind, not soon to be forgotten.

I made excuses, like it is taboo to have the "sex talk" in the Haitian culture, but my mother's actions of inviting a man into her home and giving him full reign in parenting her daughter, in my opinion, is unacceptable. I had originally felt full responsibility for my confusion and appeasing to Pierre's perversion as a child, but then I realized, *Cassandra, you are not supposed to raise yourself.* Through working with Teti, I started to gain enough clarity to hold my mother accountable for her actions. It only made sense that a mother would teach her child about good touches and bad touches and that a mother should be wary of any man who is looking after her daughter.

Still, I searched for justification for my mother's actions. I thought: *Maybe I am thinking this way because I am a social worker, and I've been educated and made aware about the prevalence of sexual abuse, and I understand the importance of such vigilant parenting.* I then spoke to a few people who confirmed that the "good touches, bad touches" lesson was taught to them, right along with "look both ways before you cross the street" and "don't talk to strangers." Brianna informed me that her father was very wary of new friends' family members, so if she were to ever sleep over a friend's house, her father would routinely ask her if she had been touched inappropriately by anyone. Micah informed me that his mother was very clear about informing his three sisters of bad touches, and taught them exactly what to do if it ever were to happen to them. In conversation with a co-worker, a woman shared that she never allowed her boyfriend to sleep in her home, because she was protective of her children. She also enforced very clear boundaries, educating her children on what was acceptable, and what was not. It became apparent that this was discussed in many homes; why had it not been discussed in mine?

I felt cheated. I felt wronged by my mother for not better preparing me, for not having a simple conversation which could have completely altered eight years of my life. I clearly remember the day when my mom told me that I was old enough to walk home by myself. I was eight years old. She said that she wouldn't be able to pick me up from school. She reminded me to look both ways before crossing the street and not to talk to any strangers. She went into detail, telling me to not trust any adult who offers me candy or an adult who has a cute puppy and asks me if I want to pet it. She told me that an adult might even say, "Something happened to your mom, and I'm here to pick you up," and my response was to immediately run and scream. She specified that if I must scream, I was to scream "FIRE" because people were more likely to pay attention. I was to take screaming seriously. No matter what, I was not to ever trust a person whom I did not recognize.

I reviewed these important lessons in my mind throughout the day, wondering why adults would ever lie and wondering why people kidnapped kids. I remember the school bells ringing and walking out of my class at the end of the day. I walked down the steps and waved goodbye to friends, as some headed to school buses, some to their parents' waiting vehicles, and others starting their trek on foot.

I looked at the open school gates, mentally preparing myself for my very first walk home by myself. I was excited, feeling like a big kid, but was also nervous. I double-checked to see if Mom or Mr. D was there, waiting for me. No one. I walked out of the schoolyard and stopped at the corner. I looked both ways, twice, just to make sure, and successfully crossed the street. I took a few more steps, and to my surprise, Mom jumped out from a car she was hiding behind. Apparently, her plans had changed, and she had been able to pick me up from school after all. She was smiling, very proud of me for doing well on my own. After that day, I walked to and from school every day, sometimes by myself and other times with my neighbor. I heeded my mother's instruction and I don't think I ever once spoke to a stranger. But what about the stranger in my home? What about the stranger who was married to my mom, who was supposed to act like my father? What do I do if he touches me inappropriately, Mom? What do I do then?

I stopped believing that my mother could read my mind as I grew older, but that particular belief was replaced with the belief in women's intuition. As I matured, I learned to trust my gut. I am a big believer that people give off certain energies and that it's important to be in touch with one's inner compass and aware of the feelings that arise within. It's like a built-in navigation system for people. There have certainly been countless times in my life when I ignored my gut feeling, usually because I allowed logic to trump my natural intuition. One could say, "It's really unfair to judge someone based on a handshake." Yet every single instance in which I ignored my inner compass, I regretfully proved that my compass had been right all along. There are people I meet who I am immediately drawn to based on their energy alone. There are others with whom, after a few seconds, I may determine that I don't share the same energy and chose not to associate. I believe all women possess this intuition, but perhaps some are more self-aware than others.

I found myself questioning my mother's intuition. I remember asking my mom to remind me of the date of my menses. It is a question typically asked on the first visit to the gynecologist, the answer to which I could never seem to remember. I learned that my mother seemed to have the same issue with memory.

She nonchalantly replied, "I don't know. Your father knows. He's the one who wrote that down."

Baffled, I replied, "How is it that Dad knows, but you don't?"

She shrugged and stated matter-of-factly, "He's the one who wrote it down."

I was infuriated by two things. One, how could she be so passive in her lack of involvement in something that one would think a mother would be interested in? And two, how is it that she saw absolutely no red flags with Pierre taking such an interest in my menses?

There was a line between fatherly and creepy. There was another occasion where Pierre insisted that everyone in the house should be bathed with a special leafy tea mix. As part of the Haitian culture, we are very superstitious people, and usually leaf baths were a measure of protection against harm. I had heard that usually babies were bathed in a special leaf bath because they are vulnerable and need to be protected. I didn't know much about it, nor why all of a sudden, everyone had to take such a bath. Apparently my father felt that it was necessary, and as usual with his decisions, it went unquestioned.

I was the last one in the house to take one of these baths. My mother and brother had each already taken one when I had gotten home that day. At that point, I was a fully-developed teenager. I didn't care about the stupid bath, but I didn't like that it was necessary for my father to pour the leafy tea mix over my head.

I stood in the doorway to my parents' room and asked my mom, "Why do we have to take this bath?"

She was lying on her bed watching TV, and passively replied, "Do what your father said. It's good and it's for your protection."

I looked at her, pleadingly, and asked, "Why don't you do it, then?"

She dismissively replied, with her eyes glued to the television, "Just let your father do it." She was irritated by my questions and didn't want to be bothered.

I stepped into the shower and crouched with my back facing my father as I wrapped my arms around my body and pressed my legs together, shielding myself from my father's gaze. He smiled and took joy in my discomfort. He actually chuckled aloud while he poured the water over my head and my body. As the leaves fell down, I remember feeling so alone. Even with my mother in the next room and my brother in his bedroom, I felt completely abandoned as I sat naked in the bathtub while my father hovered over me. I thought to myself, *This family is so fucking twisted.* Where was my mom's intuition? Did she even have any?

I made excuses for her—like "she must be overworked" or "she must be too tired"—but I remembered the incident in which she found my bra in her bedroom. I expected red flags to spring up and bells to ring in her head, but there was silence. This caused me to wonder: did she know the truth but choose to ignore it?

I didn't want to consider that as an option, but after studying social work, I have learned that denial can be a very strong defense mechanism. Denial and shame are the spokes that keep the child sexual abuse wheel going. One in four girls and one in six boys are sexually abused before the age of eighteen. Yet, parents don't want to believe that this is happening in their homes, or in their neighbors' homes, or in their family or friends' homes. People watch it on *Law & Order: Special Victims Unit*, but that's fiction, not "real life." People watch *How to Catch a Predator* and say, "There are some sick people out there. Luckily, I don't have people like that as friends or family." People watch reports of sexual abuse on primetime news and think, "This is too depressing, let me change the channel and watch something else."

Truthfully, it is a scary thought. It is terrifying to think that after tucking your kids in every night, moving into the safe suburban neighborhood, and being a good role model, someone whom you know and trust is sexually abusing your child. You don't want to think about your child's innocence being corrupted or violated. It's such an unpleasant thought that you'd rather not even entertain the idea of it. It's easier to assume that it's going on in other neighborhoods, to children of bad parents, by people who are not of your world. Instead, you stress over things like germs so that your baby doesn't get sick. Or you stress over helmets and kneepads so that your baby doesn't get a boo-boo. You stress over your baby getting kidnapped by a mysterious stranger. You worry that when your kids get older, they'll chat with strangers in an online chat room. Yet you are too terrified to consider that a predator could even exist in your own home, perhaps even despite warning signs from your inner compass.

But what about that terrified child who is hoping and praying that you'll come to his or her rescue? What about that terrified child who is far too ashamed to say anything but is begging you to see the signs, to give them an opportunity to say something? And what about that child who, day after day, becomes less and less hopeful that anyone will save him or her, and comes to the conclusion that he or she is not even worth saving? I can't help but wonder how different things could have been if *anyone*—a teacher, a relative, a counselor—had asked me at the age of five, "Cassandra, do you know the difference between a good touch and a bad touch?"

11

I don't know my mother's story; I can only speak from my own experiences with her. She is not one to talk about her past, but I've been able to gather bits of information over the years. What I do know is that she spent years of her childhood at a boarding school with nuns. My grandmother regrettably expressed being far too heavy-handed with her when she was younger, because she didn't know how else to discipline children.

Once, during a car ride while I was talking about things I was learning in class, my mother muttered that she had been physically abused as a child. I didn't explore further, but I was surprised that she expressed it in those terms. When she said it, my initial assumption was that she was referring to the traditional corporal punishment as discipline that Haitian parents commonly employ with their children. Yet I wondered, since Haitians are no strangers to corporal punishment, what made her define it as physical abuse? My parents always made it clear to Troy and I that they didn't agree with American laws and felt that spanking was a way of discipline, and it was not abuse. Did she come to a realization that it was considered abuse in America, or was it truly more than discipline and actually abuse?

Until that statement from my mother, I simply admired my grandmother for being so forward-thinking and not stuck in her old-fashioned ways. She was always interested in learning new things and new ways of seeing things. She once said to me, "You age and you learn new things. I think I was too hard on my kids. I regret that. But I grew up the same way, with a very stern aunt who was quick to pick up the belt. I see in this country, they take more time and patience with explaining things to their kids. I like that."

I had failed to consider the impact the physical abuse had had on my mother. I couldn't help but wonder how bad it was and if it had caused a traumatizing childhood for my mom, affecting her personality. Maybe that was why she always raved about how much she loved her grandmother, as opposed to her mother. She even named me after her grandma. It seemed that she, like me, had a closer relationship with her grandmother than she did with her own mother. I wondered if that might be the reason she and I had a poor relationship.

My mother recalled that when she was younger, she wasn't as close to her younger brother as I am with Troy, but it had been absolutely devastating when he died of sickle cell anemia in his thirties. It was a terrible loss. He was a doctor and a musician. I remember admiring his acoustic guitar that was always propped up in his living room whenever I would visit. I don't think she ever stopped grieving his death.

As for my biological father, I always wondered what caused him to split from my mom, but I never dared to ask her. Out of curiosity, I asked my grandmother, and she informed me that, contrary to my initial assumption that he left my mother (which was the stereotypical story with absent fathers), it was actually my mother who had left him. It turns out that he was present at the hospital when I was born, and there is a picture of him in attendance at my baptism. My grandmother only said, "Things weren't good," which caused my mom to leave him. Unfortunately, that was the only information I could gather before my grandfather ordered my grandmother to cease and desist in giving me any more information, for fear that it would somehow ruin my relationship with my parents.

My grandmother felt guilty and told me that I should ask my mom if I wanted more information. I didn't. I wondered if it was possible that whatever he did to her was something so terrible that she sees in me what she hates in him. A few years after they split, she married my stepfather, who had a daughter, Sorelle, who was only one year older than I was. I can only assume that my stepfather had poor relationships with Sorelle's mom, and then chose to marry my mom.

When I was younger, my head was filled with stories of princesses and Prince Charmings, and I asked my mother what her romantic story was. She lived in an apartment with her father in Brooklyn, New York, and my stepfather lived in the same building. She told me that she was introduced to my stepfather by her dad. I asked about the proposal, and she matter-of-factly said that he just asked her to marry him. I got the impression that it was an arrangement: he needed a wife and she needed a husband. From what I saw, the marriage wasn't a very romantic one. My mother and stepfather referred to each other with terms of endearment, such as "cherie" in French, or "honey" in English. There was a peck on the lips or cheek as they entered or left the home. The gender roles were very clear. She was responsible for the cooking and cleaning, and he was responsible for mowing the lawn and paying the bills. It was like an arrangement, and they seemed complacent with it.

My mother once said to me that she was depressed. I dismissed it as another work-related complaint, but what if she really meant it? She had gone to school to become a Licensed Practical Nurse, so she must have studied depression. Maybe she really was depressed. My mother's job at the nursing home was endlessly stressful. She described her elderly and dying patients cursing at her and calling her by racial slurs. "Thank-you's" were rare and management was unbearable. There was a constant fear of liability if a client were to fall or become bruised. She had to do heavy lifting, roll patients over or transfer them from one bed to another, change diapers, and clean messes. The night shift wasn't necessarily a perk, either. She had taken the night shift for when Troy and I were younger so that she would be available to be home when we got back from school. She got into the routine, and even after we got older, she kept the night shift.

After work, she would return to a patriarchal home in which she was the sole person responsible for grocery shopping, cooking and cleaning. My father didn't so much as boil water. She made him breakfast, packed his lunch for work and cooked dinner. Sometimes she would work an eleven-to-seven shift at the nursing home, and then work seven to three at another agency. During her down time, she found succor in her bed, often referred to as her "throne," until she fell asleep. In the end, I don't know my mother's story; I can only speak from my own experiences with her.

⁂

"What will you miss?" I was asked. The question was in reference to the possibility that my mother would not believe me. The answer was not a simple one. Such a response from my mother would result in the end of an already delicate relationship. It would be the ultimate betrayal. I was seventy percent sure that she would not believe me. Yet, despite the fact that the negatives outweighed the positives, I held on to that thirty percent. I would hold onto and cherish all positive experiences, like a child who would clench onto their last wrinkled dollar at an arcade, waiting until they would find the most special of all games, worthy of spending their last dollar. The real question was: what was I holding on to?

Societally, it is unacceptable to have a poor relationship with one's mother. No matter what, a mother is held in the highest regard, and if you don't see your mom that way, then something's wrong with you. Whenever I complained to friends about my poor relationship with my mother, the response was typically, "Well you should just accept her the way she is," or "She's your mom; she loves you, even if she doesn't show it" or "Maybe you should take the initiative and find a way to fix it." It was as if the definition of 'mom' being equivalent to 'loving' was as absolute of an equation as the sum of one plus one is two. It also seemed that a mother is always flawless, and on the rare occasion that she is flawed, then it was excusable because after all, she is a mother and would forever hold that title.

"You shouldn't date a guy who says he doesn't get along with his own mom." I had heard this statement many times. Hence, it was common thinking that a person's relationship to one's mom determines their relationship with others. This went as far back as Freud's Oedipal Complex theory. As a matter of fact, I found it very important that Micah had a great relationship with his own mother, but mostly because I wanted to have a great relationship with her. I don't think that it was societal pressure that kept me holding on to the idea of a good relationship with my mom. It was the idea that of all the people in this world, the woman who gave birth to me should accept me. Despite the fact that I discovered that friends can be like family, being rejected by my mother would be unlike any rejection I would ever face again in my life. I preferred the idea of having a bad mother as opposed to having no mother at all.

I imagined the birth of my first child. I saw myself laying in the hospital bed with Micah on my right side. In the waiting room would be my brother, my friends, his mother and siblings. Despite the love and support from those people in my life, the absence of my mother would be poignant. I imagined my children coming home from school, having to do a project on their grandparents, like I had to do in second grade, and their cute little faces looking up at me and saying, "Mommy, why do we only have one grandma?" What would I say to that? Yes, my relationship with my mother was a poor one, but the rejection that I was possibly facing would be felt for the rest of my life.

Sometimes I felt like an orphan shopping for a mom. I would go to my friends' homes and imagine what it would be like if I had their mothers instead of my own. At Brianna's home, after a night out, I would awaken to the smell of bacon. Her mother would be in the kitchen with an apron, asking me if I had enjoyed myself the night before. She usually would see Brianna and me in our outfits before we left the house to go to dinner, a birthday party, or a night on the town. She would demand that we take lots of pictures, to be shared over breakfast the next morning. We'd sit in the kitchen for hours and discuss the events of the night before, while Brianna's mother prepared breakfast. While eating, we would chat about current events, both personal and worldly.

When I'd visit my high-school friend Keket, I felt completely at home in her house. There would be Kompa music playing in the background while she, her mother, her uncle and I discussed various things. Sometimes her uncle would grill delicious food. We ladies drank wine while he had rum on the rocks. We would engage in political discussions, conspiracy theories, racial conversation, topics related to Haiti, or "bay blague" (which is telling Haitian jokes). I would spend hours there, feeling completely at home. I admired the relationship that Keket had with her mother. They were almost like sisters. Sometimes I would just watch their interactions with one another. At times they would argue, but more importantly, they *knew* each other. Keket's mother knew who Keket was, Keket knew who her mother was, and they were comfortable in knowing one another.

I paid particular attention to Micah's mother, the woman who would hopefully soon be my mother-in-law. Like her son, it was impossible not to love her. Her personality alone could light up a room. We had spoken quite a few times either via telephone or via Micah, and although I hadn't yet met her in person, I was immediately drawn to her personality. Micah's mother is sort of like the Godmother of the family. She's the matriarch. I respected her ability to raise five wonderful kids after the untimely death of her husband due to cancer. She is very assertive and confident but is very loving and nurturing. She has a very wise air about her, and it appeared that one should always listen if she had something to say. She's not only Micah's mother but also his best friend.

Micah would refer to her by her first name, Coral. When he spoke to Coral, he was able to speak to her like he would've spoken to his father, or with one of his male friends. They were able to have very blunt conversations about relationships, sex, and life altogether. During one of their conversations, Micah revealed to his mom that I hated my father and that he was a very controlling individual. After some thought, she replied, "He did something to her."

"What do you mean?" Micah asked.

"There's something I don't like about that man. For a daughter to say that she hates her father, he must've done something to her. Something's not right there."

When Micah relayed the story to me, I was so surprised that, with such a little bit of information, his mother was able to come to such an accurate conclusion. Oddly, I wasn't upset at her being on the brink of knowing my personal situation; instead, I was impressed. I was amazed that she had so much intuition. Even if she had been wrong, she was a woman who asked questions when flags appeared, and I respected her for that. Later on in a different conversation, Micah revealed to his mom that my father was not my biological father. This raised further suspicion in Coral, causing her to wonder if he touched me inappropriately. At that point, Micah did not fully know my story, but a short while later his mother's intuitive statements would become clearer to him.

Before we started dating, I had told Micah when going to therapy was just a thought; I didn't tell him the particulars, but

I gave him a vague notion that I had things to work out. He was extremely supportive, expressing that he admired my ability to face my demons and that it required much inner strength. When we started dating, I felt that I trusted him enough to let him in on why I was seeing Teti. I told him that part of my reason for seeing Teti was because of Mr. D. I was tentative in telling him this for fear that his view of me would change. Not only did I struggle with the shame that I felt, but more so, I didn't want my sexual abuse to define who I was. I didn't want Micah to stop seeing me as the strong-willed, happy and loving woman and to start seeing me as a poor and helpless victim. I predicted a sad reaction, and I could not tolerate the thought of him pitying me. There is something about pity that makes me think about a frightened, feeble, incapable animal. One to which you shake your head at, avert your eyes, and say, "Tsk, tsk, tsk, poor thing." Yet I took the risk and told him about Mr. D.

The way I felt about Micah, I knew it was necessary that he know what was going on with me. It would be unfair to him otherwise. I was in love with him and I saw a future with him. My story about Mr. D was a test, a precursor for the big story about my father. If he couldn't handle Mr. D, then he wouldn't be able to handle my father. He listened intently. I could hear sadness in his voice as he asked me a few questions. Afterwards, there was an awkward silence. I was scared. Had I shared too much? Was this too much for him to handle? Does he feel obligated to somehow "save me?" He sensed the awkwardness and reassured me that he did not see me any differently. Naturally, he was sad about what happened but was happy that I was addressing it. I informed him that somebody else had also sexually abused me, and that in time, he would discover who.

12

Micah and I had conversation after conversation in which I alluded to the mystery man who had sexually abused me. I ended up even confusing myself in referring to how devastated *that* family would be if I were to disclose the sexual abuse. The endless pronoun use in trying to hide what was obviously my family became tiring. I was running circles on the track. Even Teti assumed, "Cassandra, I'm sure he's figured it out."

Finally, mid-conversation, frustrated at my inability to speak openly and honestly, I asked him, "Do you have any idea who this person is?"

He replied, "Yes, but I will wait until you feel comfortable telling me."

I slapped my palm to my forehead and let out a burst of laughter and shook my head. I imagined him smiling to himself on the other end of the line. I immediately felt foolish that I had gone through great lengths to conceal the identity of my abuser to him, yet I felt the freeing release that is often felt after coming home from a long workday, and shedding the suffocating and confining corporate garments.

Considering that I had once considered myself a fairly good liar (or was I?), I was curious as to what gave me away.

Apparently, the apple didn't fall far from the tree. Micah came to the conclusion that the only person that made sense was my father; it was the most common scenario. To him it was obvious. It felt so much more comfortable with the truth out in the open and being able to speak to Micah about my struggles. My thoughts and emotions poured out of me, as river water would pour past a broken dam. He was a person I could lean on when I wasn't speaking to Teti. He was understanding when I was seemingly angry for no reason or overwhelmed with thoughts about my disclosure on top of school, work and internship.

As usual, one day I went to work from eight in the morning to four in the afternoon, then went home and ate an early dinner, and then got on the train for the hour-long ride to the city for my late night seminar. This particular seminar was all about the licensure for social work. I sat and took notes, paying attention to the pre-approval application and fee, as well as the exam itself that cost over $300. The exam was also notoriously devious and complex with a sixty-percent failure rate on the first try. (Graduate school didn't actually prepare you for the licensing exam. *Go figure.*) Then there was the issue of the lack of reciprocity between states with licensure. That meant that even if I passed my exam and got my license in New Jersey, I might have to apply again in Georgia. Not to mention, I had to prepare for graduation.

Obstacles were surrounding me like jagged mountains around a ravine, and clawing my way up and over the sheer cliffs seemed futile—utterly hopeless. I kept myself together in the classroom, but as I rode home on the train, tears gushed down my face as I sobbed into my hands. All of the stress that I was pushing down inside me had erupted; it finally reached its boiling point and had nowhere else to go but my eyeballs.

On top of that, I had been denied a promotion at my job due to favoritism. The girl who got the position was not only less experienced then I was but also had only been on the job for half the time that I'd been there. All that mattered was that she made best friends out of her supervisor, as well as other supervisors in the office. They would get drunk, party and go on trips together, while I maintained clear and professional boundaries with my supervisors. After the rejection, and having to change the diapers of the girl who had now become my supervisor, I had had enough. I no longer wanted to work at a job that didn't appreciate me, and going into work every day became intolerable.

At internship, I didn't feel that I was doing as well as I could have been. I was making documentation mistakes and couldn't seem to get the gist of all of the policies and procedures even after months of being there. All of the clinicians had average caseloads of seventy clients and seemed to work like well-oiled machines. I, on the other hand, felt immensely incompetent in such a fast-paced environment. We were expected to see clients back to back; yet, heaps of documentation needed to be handwritten for each client. I was overwhelmed.

Symptoms of anxiety infected my wellbeing and seized control of my functions. There were times when I felt my chest tighten up as if there were a large, cement slab pinning me down. Other times, my arms and fingertips would tingle as if my blood had stopped circulating altogether. My heart would beat out of my chest for no apparent reason, and my stomach felt like someone was wringing it out. On many occasions, my fellow intern looked at me with a concerned expression as I sat at my desk, intently focused on the deep breathing technique that I had instructed to clients so many times as a relaxation tool to combat anxiety. The seven-day workweek had become draining. These symptoms washed over me without warning, like a summer's mid-day thundershower, and the feelings were frustrating within themselves.

I had a forty-hour workweek Sunday through Thursday, a twenty-one hour internship four times a week, including all day Friday, and school all day Saturday. My social life was nonexistent. I spent most of my day, from morning to night, outside of my home. I was lucky to stay up long enough to exchange a few words with Micah or Brianna before I fell asleep at night.

Meanwhile, I was dealing with feelings related to moving to a foreign place. As much as I was in love with Micah, I felt tremendous fear of adapting to a completely new environment and the sudden change in the dynamic of the relationship from long-distance to sharing the same quarters. On top of it all, the disclosure of my sexual abuse lingered like some trace chemical in the atmosphere—ever-present and inescapable.

It was too much. Never before in my life did I feel so distraught; I was at my nadir. I felt completely lost in a large, dark ocean, and I couldn't see the shoreline. I wanted nothing more than for the waves to carry me far, far away from my reality. There were countless times when I would close my eyes and wish that I was dreaming and that my life was all just a nightmare, an evil trick. I wished I would wake up and have a *normal* life, with a *normal* family—one where I wouldn't have to deal with or face all of my problems.

That night, after the seminar, I realized that I couldn't run away from the cold, hard, and very tangible reality that I was living, and the tears just flowed. Micah had called me to say goodnight but was greeted with his sobbing girlfriend on the other end of the line.

I felt like I was drowning. I wanted to drown. I wanted to stop everything and just disappear—disappear beneath the waves and cease to exist. I was struggling to hold my head above the waters but I just wanted to take a break from life. I had a pair of scissors in my room, and I began toying with the idea of cutting myself with them. I told him that I wanted to feel physical pain, anything to distract myself from the immense emotional pain inside of me. Micah cried with me and for me, and he reminded me of all of the reasons I was working so hard and what I wanted to see in my future. It was difficult to focus on the future when the present was so unbearable, but he stayed on the phone with me until I allowed my exhaustion to carry me to a dreamless sleep.

My depression stuck with me for weeks. I was a zombie; I was numb, simply fulfilling the bare essentials of my work requirements. Tears came easily, too easily. Any minute stressor, from a disagreement with a friend to being reprimanded by a supervisor, would cause me to end the day with puffy eyes and a face full of tears. I became more aware that my body would betray me and react, even when I tried desperately to conceal the emotions that were coursing through my veins, right beneath my skin. I became frustrated. I had never been one to be easily rattled, and I felt that over time, instead of getting stronger with therapy, I was exerting signs of weakness.

I reached a point in which I felt desolate and broken down. I no longer wanted to spend hours on the phone crying to Micah, nor did I want to cry myself to sleep alone at night. I don't know if my body grew tired of producing tears or if the depression simply started to wear off, but over time, the spontaneous crying spells stopped and I became better able to function. Even without the tears, though, every day was a struggle to keep myself from unraveling. All I could do was put one foot in front of the other, focusing on what I needed to accomplish, digging myself out of my depression—keeping my eyes on the carrot.

Not long after my emotional breakdown, I was fired from my job. Initially, I was devastated, but was soon overcome by a sense of calm. Although I felt that the layoff was biased, my prayers for salvation had been answered in the most unexpected way. I now had time to focus my attention on school. I increased my weekly hours at my internship, ensuring that I would attain all of the hours necessary for graduation. I also saw it as an opportunity to start studying for my licensing exam, which I was terribly apprehensive about. Having worked since the age of fifteen, I never would've foreseen that I would be happy to get fired from a job. Yet, at that point in my life, when my mental wellness was at risk, it was a true blessing in disguise.

During one of our many conversations about the future, I discussed with Micah how sad it would be if neither of my parents would be at our wedding. His response indicated that I was being dramatic in making such a statement. I was surprised. He went further to explain that my father may not be walking me down the aisle but could at least still attend the wedding. Such a statement prompted me to ask, "What do you think my father actually did to me?"

Micah proceeded to share how he was under the impression that what my father had was an illness. He saw him as a sick man who struggled with boundaries. I was astounded. I didn't even know how to respond. Micah elaborated, "I try to find the good in people. He can't be all bad. There must be some good in your father."

I wasn't sure what to tell him, but it was very clear that Micah did not know the extent of what my father did to me. I felt that I was back at square one with my disclosure to Micah.

At that stage in therapy, I had started writing in a journal. As a student of social work, and as a client of Dr. Teti, I knew that it was best for me to face my uncomfortable thoughts about my father. Yet, I still did not want those intrusive thoughts to be a part of my regular journal. Writing them down was difficult to begin with, so I wanted them to be easily disposed of. I wrote them down on a separate piece of paper, which I tucked away in my journal.

I felt that this was an opportunity for me to share with Micah what I had written. I read my journal entry aloud to him:

"I was reminded of Tales from the Crypt today. I remember the episode in which the woman hit a hitchhiker and he haunts her, repeatedly saying, 'Thanks for the ride lady.' That terrified me as a kid. I wonder if my brother remembers that one. One of my first

*memories was of watching Tales from the Crypt with
my father late at night while my brother was asleep.
Nothing happened that night, but it was the beginning
of many late night movies."*

"This was when you were five years old?" interrupted Micah.
"Yes," I replied.
"Wow. He was a bad father," exclaimed Micah.
Perplexed as to the reasoning for such an obvious statement, I asked, "Why do you say that?"
"Because, he let you stay up to watch scary movies at the age of five. That's a bad parent."
My stomach dropped as memories of our previous conversation inundated my mind. *There's no way he didn't know.* I became more blunt in my statements: "Ummm, well *Tales from the Crypt* only turned into porn later on."
"He showed you porn?!" he exclaimed. "Wow, I figured he had boundary issues...like wanting to bathe you after you were too old, or touching you inappropriately. I saw him as a person who had a sort of mental illness, like a defect, and was otherwise a decent human being." He paused. "I—I didn't know that he was an evil person who tried to corrupt you by showing you porn as a little girl...like he saw your innocence and intentionally broke it down in order to accomplish his sick agenda." I let him ruminate aloud. After some silence, with resolve, he sighed, "He is an evil man."
I didn't know what to make of it. I wondered why Micah thought I was so distraught for all this time. I figured that he understood that my father was not Mr. D. He was far worse.
I listened to him on the phone, trying to decipher his impression of the entire situation. I thought: *yes, pedophilia is a sick disease, causing the people afflicted by it to have an uncontrollable attraction to children. But pedophiles are predators, who find ways to lure their prey through bribes, manipulation, and sometimes force. They use their power as adults to*

take advantage of trusting children. The same way a handy-man has the proper tools for his trade in his tool-kit, so do pedophiles. The difference is that the tools used by a pedophile are both visible and invisible. They use emotional tools, such as power, special attention, bribery, and brainwashing. Their visible tools appear harmless—a warm smile, candy, videog-ames, or adorable pets. Despite the fact that they have an ill-ness, their behaviors are inexcusable.

"My father knew exactly what he was doing," I said to Micah, confirming his statement that Pierre was indeed an evil man. He made calculated and conscious decisions year after year in order to fulfill his sick fantasies. I had allowed Micah to deduce that it was my father who had sexually abused me, but such a passive decision caused Micah to assume that, similar to Mr. D, the abuse at the hands of my father was minimal and in-frequent. Micah and I exchanged our good nights, and hung up the phone. Yet I knew that the conversation was far from over.

The next day, I had an appointment with Teti. I explained that although I was frustrated that Micah did not grasp the magnitude of the situation, I did not want to clarify it. I did not want to tell him how far things had gone. Maybe the fact that he could not surmise what had happened to me was an indication that he was unable to handle the reality of the abuse.

Teti firmly said to me, "If Micah truly loves you, if you lived it, then he can hear it."

This is also the same thing she said to me about disclosing the truth to my mother. Those words resonated in me, but there was a strong struggle inside. The relief I had initially felt was replaced with apprehension.

What if he became disgusted with me? What if it affect-ed the way he saw me intimately? He might not ever want to touch me again or look at me the in the same light. What if he no longer saw me as the beautiful woman whom he loved and wanted to marry? What if his image of me changed to that of a girl whom he loved but for whom he could no longer feel any attraction? What if he couldn't get past the sadness, pity or revulsion?

This was my biggest fear. Would my mark of Cain show itself, revolting Micah from me forever? It was evident that I was avoiding, but Teti's words came back to me. I lived it, so Micah can hear it.

As I walked to my car from Teti's office, I convinced myself to dial his number. I lived it, and he loves me, so he can handle it. He answered on the second ring.

"Hi, baby."

He sounded happy, and I didn't want to sink the mood, to drag him down to my depths.

"Hey, Micah." The words dripped from my mouth.

"What's wrong?" he immediately asked. After relying on each other's voices for so long, he was quick to notice any emotional change in my voice.

"Remember the conversation we had last night?" I started.

"Yes," Micah replied.

I was tentative. "Well...It made me realize that you aren't fully aware of what my father did to me."

The tone in his voice changed. "Uh-huh," he replied, indicating that I should go on.

I pushed myself along. "I talked to Teti, and she said that you should know what really happened."

He replied imploringly, "Are you ready to tell me?" He sensed the hesitation in my voice, and sounded nervous.

"I don't know."

I was chickening out, as the feeling of shame fell over me. But I knew it was too late; I had already started the ball rolling. Still, I tried to change the subject.

I had a craving for something to munch on and had stopped into a convenience store. I was browsing through the candy aisle with the phone to my ear. In a chipper voice, I asked, "Do you think I should pick up a Snickers bar or a bag of M&Ms? I can't choose." Before he could answer, I prattled, "Well, I haven't had a Snickers for a while, so I think I'm gonna get that one. This is a reminder that I should probably work out more since I keep eating so poorly."

Silence.

I continued rambling in a nervously cheerful voice, "Maybe I'll start back up to the gym again...but their monthly fees are crazy. I just need the motivation to run on the treadmill because I am so out of shape it's ridiculous."

I had just gotten back to my car, candy in hand, when large fat raindrops hit my windshield. It started pouring outside, and I thought how lucky I was to have gotten in the car before the downpour. It was raining so hard that the sound of the raindrops hitting the metal hood of my car was deafening, yet it was distinctly silent on the other end of the line.

"Micah?" I asked.

"Yes?" he replied.

"Why are you so quiet?"

"I'm waiting for you to tell me what you called me to tell me," he said patiently.

I was frustrated; I didn't want to have to say the words out loud. I yelled, "Dammit, Micah! Why don't you know? I mean, how could you not know?"

Defensive, he responded, "I don't know. You never outright told me, so I could only guess."

"Well guess then! You know it's more than boundaries. Just guess!" I yelled, as I rested my forehead on the steering wheel of my parked car.

"I don't know," Micah said cautiously.

"Guess!" I beseeched him.

"Did he have sex with you?"

I literally stopped breathing. How do you just say "Yes" to a question like that? I knew that he would guess it but I still didn't want to discuss it.

"Hello?" he asked.

"Yeah..." I responded.

"So your father had sex with you," he clarified.

"Yup!" I squeezed out the nonchalant-sounding answer out from the air that had been trapped in my lungs. My entire body was tense. I stuck my finger in one ear to dull out the sound of torrential rain hitting the roof of my car. I listened intently to the sounds on the other end. At first I only heard the dull electrical buzzing sound coming from the phone. I then heard Micah's breathing on the other end. I heard a shuffle as he presumably shifted in his seat. I heard the sounds of cars driving by. I silently begged him to say something, anything. We sat in silence for what seemed like hours. My muscles started to ache from my body being so tense. I shut my eyes, and prayed, *Dear God, please...*

"That man is the devil," he muttered, breaking the silence. "He is a pure evil person, to rob you the way he has." The quiver in his voice revealed that he had started to cry.

In a quiet voice, I asked, "Does this change the way you see me?" I braced myself for the answer.

"No!" He assured. I listened intently for any sign of pity, or a polite answer to satisfy me. He continued, "On the contrary, I better appreciate your ability to have such positive energy, and your ability to love. It's amazing that you are such a positive person after all you went through. He tried to take your light away from you, but your light continues to shine in spite of what he did to you."

I listened in silence.

He continued further, his voice filled with emotion, "Your mother should have protected you. The way things work in my family is that we do not allow any negativity around us. You are my family now, Cassandra, and I will protect you. No matter what happens with your mom, you have your home right here, with me. We will start our family together, free of any poison."

An audible cry startled me as it escaped my lips. I was besieged with emotion. I had never cried out of complete joy before.

I blurted, "I was afraid you would be grossed out by me," as I wiped my tears. "I thought you wouldn't love me anymore, and see me as a damaged person, but instead you show me more love? Instead you focus on all of the good you see in me?"

I was dumbfounded.

"Baby, I can't blame you for the things that you have gone through. You have amazed me with your strength in going to see Teti, and your strength in deciding to finally take back your life and tell your mother the truth. I can't tell you what kind of person I would be if I were in your situation. I would've probably blackmailed him, had him buy me a new car, and made his life a living Hell. Yet, you...you are different."

The rain began to let up, and I smiled through my tears, "There have been times when I have thought of that, but there was something about it that made it feel like I was selling my body in a way. I couldn't take money from him. Plus—lucky me—I believe in karma. I swear if I didn't believe in karma, I would be a really vengeful badass bitch."

He laughed.

I asked, "Does this make you understand things a little better with me?"

He admitted, "Well, I certainly understand why you hate your father so much. And also why you prefer to be avoidant."

"What do you mean?" I asked, curious.

"Well, you have spent most of your life suppressing something so dark deep inside you. You have lived your life walking on a fine line, on eggshells. Now I get why you avoid conflict. You avoid uncomfortable situations to keep the peace."

I felt so happy and blessed to have Micah in my life. He understood me profoundly, and to my core. His reaction to my disclosure made me feel a much stronger faith in him. I expected the worst, but instead got an even better response than I ever imagined. He shattered my belief of carrying the mark of Cain to smithereens. I felt relieved of the ugly mark. I had never thought of myself in the way that he did.

I never considered myself to be a warm and loving person in spite of my sexual abuse. Instead, I would always focus on my faults and flaws because of my sexual abuse. A new light shone on me; when I looked in the mirror, I saw someone new. For the first time, I truly believed that I could be loved, something that I never thought would be genuinely possible. This is why I never showed anyone all sides of me before; I feared that people weren't equipped to love me for everything that I was and everything that I had been through. But on that day, I realized that another person could indeed truly love me, wholly, the way that a prince would love a princess. Micah didn't know this, but his words were engraved in my soul and would continue to stay there forever.

13

M icah was scheduled to visit. On the table was a discussion about whether or not he should attend dinner with my parents and me. Micah was torn. He felt that he had absolutely nothing to prove to my father. He didn't want to look him in the eye or shake his hand, let alone be in the same room with him. At the same token, he felt that as my boyfriend, he had a responsibility to demonstrate to my family that he was a respectable man. He still had to make a positive impression. By him treating my father poorly for no apparent reason, Micah would be perceived as rude and disrespectful. I listened to him in amazement as he described his dilemma to me. It was the same struggle that I had endured for years.

I would argue with myself: *Cassandra, should you treat this man like he deserves to be treated, curse him out, and get painted as an evil person as a result, or should you just play your role as the daughter and greet him cordially with a smile to keep the peace?* This was an everyday dilemma that I faced. This is also why I avoided my father altogether; then I didn't have to make the decision.

It was amazing to hear Micah speak firsthand about something that I had always experienced alone and in silence. On the weekend that Micah came to visit, after our conversation, we decided that he was not yet ready to see my parents and play nice. Instead, I planned to spend the weekend with him in a hotel and go on fun dates, of course without my parent's knowledge—I would have to say I was staying with a friend.

The day before his flight was scheduled to arrive, I received a text message from Pierre while I was at my internship. It stated: "Tomorrow night I am having prayers in the house from 7pm to 3am. It's going to be a little noisy and a few people are coming. So, think about sleeping over your friend's house."

First, I shrugged, "How perfect, I wasn't planning on being home anyway."

I immediately texted my brother to see if he received the same text. He had, and was already in the process of making plans. Then the curiosity set in as I reread the text message.

What was going on? The year before, my father had gotten mysteriously ill. For two days, he had a pounding headache, vomiting, diarrhea, and was unable to get out of bed. He had no warning symptoms; as a matter of fact, the illness seemed very sudden. He went to the doctor, who informed him that he could not find anything wrong with him. When you tell a superstitious Haitian that he is ill, without any explanation, it is automatically assumed that there are malicious and supernatural factors involved.

Two nights after his doctor's appointment, I had arrived home from work to see a yellow taxicab outside of my house. It stood out of place in my driveway; like a flamingo in Manhattan, the yellow cab was incongruous with the quiet suburbs. As I opened the front door, my nostrils were greeted with a noticeable smell of incense. The distinct sound of men chanting met my ears, as their redundant raucity crept upstairs from the basement and through the walls. I went upstairs to find my brother playing video games in his room. He had no answers as to what was going on. Both of my parents' cars were in the driveway, but they were not in their room, nor were they in the kitchen. I assumed that they were downstairs with the strange men who were producing such booming sounds. I didn't dare go downstairs to find out.

I knew that my father was more superstitious than what is typical for a Haitian. He was cautious about donating his clothes or going to the barber to get his haircut. He spoke about evildoers putting spells on others by attaining personal artifacts, and accessing the victim via food or even dreams. I assumed that the stories I had heard about voodoo ceremonies were limited the countryside of Haiti, but I would've never guessed that one would occur in Central Jersey. I figured that people left their ceremonies and rituals in the home country, but apparently it crossed the oceans, along with the superstition.

I'll never forget the incident in which father was telling a voodoo story to other family members, and I had muttered under my breath, "I don't believe in that stuff." After all, I was raised Catholic, and if you don't believe in something, then it can't hurt you, right?

He looked me dead in my eyes, with such austerity, pointing his finger. "Do not speak on what you know nothing about," he said. His eyes penetrated me as if I had made a personal insult before he continued his story.

It made me uneasy that there were *hougan* in my home. Hougan is Haitian Creole for voodoo priest, or witch doctor. I knew that had my grandmother been visiting, she would not have tolerated such non-Christian worship. I was surprised that my mother, having been raised by my grandmother and a product of Catholic school, would condone something like this happening in her home.

I didn't understand my father's inclination towards voodoo, nor did I want to understand. I didn't want any part of what was going on. Unfortunately, I didn't have much say about our visitors' presence. Therefore, I went into my room, shut the door, and put the TV on the loudest possible volume in order to drown out the chanting coming from downstairs.

A few days later, my father's symptoms abated. Whether it was due to the natural course of the illness, or due to his special ritual, I'll never know.

One year later, it was happening again. When I received that text from my father, my first assumption was that he was trying to remedy something. But nobody, as far as I knew, was ill. I became suspicious and thought that it was far too coincidental that it was only a few months before my plan to disclose the sexual abuse.

I was very curious as to the agenda of this "prayer." Was it malicious in nature, or was he seeking protection? But in the process of seeking protection for himself, would that mean that there was harm coming my way? And why would my brother and I need to leave the house? What about this ceremony was any different than the previous one? Why were the times so specific and why for so long? What was the significance of "3am"? Would my mom be involved in the ceremony?

Maybe, as a means of protection, he was finding a way to lock my mom down, to affix her to him with invisible chains. It made sense; he didn't cook, he was going blind with his glaucoma, and he was getting old, so why not?

On the night of the "prayers," as my father called them, I drove by the house out of curiosity, to see if I could get a glimpse of what was going on. Micah and I were exhausted after spending the day in New York, dining in Manhattan, and going to the Bronx Zoo. By the time we returned to Jersey, it was nightfall. I craned my neck and squinted through the passenger window as we crept by my house in my car. I expected the downstairs lights to be on, limiting the ceremony to the first floor, but as I drove by, a green glow coming from the living room upstairs. There were also *two* taxicabs in the driveway. A feeling of uneasiness gripped my heart, sending a quiver through my body.

I kept driving and pulled into the gas station nearby. As an attendant pumped my gas, I started panicking. I thought: *Two taxi cabs? Who knows how many of the hougan are there. Whatever they're doing is on a much larger scale than I thought. Why are they in the whole house? What if they are in my room? And why is there a green glow coming from upstairs? That's just bizarre and eerie.* I felt like I was in the Twilight Zone, and the gas attendant would return with a pig's snout for a nose.

Micah sat quietly and patiently in the passenger seat as I racked my brain to recall details from the previous time. There had been voices of many men—loud enough to carry up to my bedroom upstairs—who had apparently arrived in only one taxicab. Seeing two taxicabs was highly disturbing, because I could only wonder how much strength or power my father was seeking from these people—and why. With that many men, I was convinced that their ceremony was covering the entire house.

The gas attendant informed me that my tank was filled. His normalness was a reminder that the supernatural events occurring down the street had not permeated the house to taint the rest of the world. I decided to drive by one more time, just to make sure that the lights were off in my room and my brother's room.

I passed by again, this time more slowly, and I had a better view, now looking through the driver's side window. On approach, I noticed that the motion-sensor lights had been activated in the driveway. My eyes quickly darted to a third taxicab as it pulled in front of my house. I sped away as I noticed Pierre stepping out onto the doorstep to greet whoever arrived in the third cab, for fear that he would recognize my car or me. I was relieved to spot that both my room and my brother's rooms were still dark. Yet the third taxicab left me even more rattled. Assuming that each person rode solo, there was a minimum of three men, but wouldn't they all just catch a ride together? They did last time. So there was a maximum of twelve people in my house, and I had no idea what they were up to. I was certainly spooked.

I said to myself, "Of course, only in the life of Cassandra Baptiste does she drive by her home with glowing green lights and taxicabs full of voodoo priests. Next thing I know, the house will be floating."

I apologized to Micah for the absolute insanity of the things going on in my life and commended him for not running out of the car at his first opportunity. He informed me that, being a part of a West Indian family himself, uncustomary methods to address illnesses were not uncommon. He suggested that maybe my father sensed the negative energy present in the home, and felt it necessary to cleanse it. Or maybe he was experiencing pedophile-like feelings towards my cousins and wanted to cleanse himself. None of the theories or assumptions put me at ease.

I was grateful to be in a good place in my relationship with God. Had this happened a few years earlier, I would have been terrified because my faith had been irresolute. At this point, although I found faults in the Catholic Church, I found peace with my faith in God. I didn't go to church every Sunday, but I found solace in speaking to God on my own terms. I was thankful that our hotel maintained the custom of keeping the Bible in each room. I figured a few extra prayers couldn't hurt.

When we returned to the hotel room, I immediately reached for the Bible. I remembered that when I was younger, my grandmother had me memorize Psalm 23. It is a psalm for protection. I was upset at myself that I had forgotten it due to lack of reciting it over the years.

I read aloud: "*The LORD is my shepherd; I shall not want. He makes me to lie down in green pastures; He leads me beside the still waters...*" I read two other psalms meant for protection. Micah sat across from me and listened reverently.

When I finished reading the last psalm, Micah asked me if I would like him to pray with me. Although kneeling is not customary in the Baptist religion, Micah kneeled next to me and held my hand as we prayed together. I felt that we had reached another level of intimacy. We certainly had our differences with me identifying as Catholic and he identifying as Baptist, but holding hands in prayer, we transcended the menial disagreements between religious institutions and reach a level of united faith.

The next day, after I dropped off Micah at the airport, I emptied a small water bottle and filled it with holy water from my church. When I returned to my house, I felt a perturbing emptiness. My mother was tidying up the dining room, and the curtains were wide open, letting the bright white sunlight in. It swirled around the house like thick smoke, illuminating all corners of the home. It was unnatural, since Father was quite particular about having the blinds drawn for privacy. She nonchalantly asked me how my weekend was, to which I responded, "Fine." She was dallying around, organizing things in the home with a smile on her face, as if nothing had happened the night before. All that was missing was a French maid's outfit and a feather duster to complete the scene.

There was an undeniable sense of eeriness in the house. It was too clean. After surveying my room to ensure that everything was in its correct place, I dared to explore downstairs. The room downstairs—which had been previously cluttered with boxes, bins, books, broken fans, old appliances, and dysfunctional TV sets—was now completely empty aside from the treadmill and the bookshelf, which were pushed against the wall. The floor was spotless. There was no evidence of those items ever being there. I felt like I was in a movie—in one of those flashback scenes where the screen turns black and white and the protagonist finds herself standing in the same place, but in the distant past. I couldn't imagine what had gone on in that room the night before. I didn't dare take one step in, not without my holy water. I pushed open the door to the adjacent bathroom, and saw what looked like ashes floating in the toilet water.

I ventured down the hall into the den, and there were extra chairs pulled out, arranged in a half-circle. Again, the eerie empty feeling lingered, as if things were missing, as if a person had done too well of a job cleaning up after their crimes. I imagined strange men in the seats. Were they tall or short, scary-looking or friendly, relaxed or stern? I wondered what they sat around and talked about—the weather? Sports? What do you talk about after you do a voodoo ceremony? Or was this where the ceremony took place?

I cautiously walked around the chairs, making sure that I did not touch them, and proceeded up the back stairs. Along the base of the back door leading to the porch, there was a straight line of crumbled-up black particles, which looked like the same burnt ashes in the toilet bowl. I saw it again, smeared on the walls in the upstairs bathroom.

There was an overwhelming smell of incense throughout the home; it had been absorbed into the walls and floorboards. I sprayed my room and my brother's room with the holy water while reading scriptures from the Bible. I was armed and on guard for any spiritual warfare.

The next weekend, as I got ready for church, which I attended alone, I ran into my parents on my way out. "Where are you coming from," I asked with curiosity. "We just came from church," they casually replied, as if it were an ordinary occurrence. I pondered to myself: *Is that how it works? Voodoo ceremony one weekend and a Roman Catholic mass the next weekend?* I lost a little bit more faith in my mother. She truly disappointed me this time.

14

The next day, my brother and I were hanging in my room, while my parents were away at work, discussing our individual relationships with our parents, or lack thereof. Troy held a lot of animosity towards our father due to his dictator-like ways of running a home and lack of respect for Troy as a human being. As a result, Troy had no respect for our father.

Instead, Troy carried reverence for our neighbor, Tony. Tony was an All-American veteran who had Italian roots. He was often outside his house, smoking a cigarette. He had a welcoming smile and a strong New York accent. It was easy to strike up conversation with him. He was always ready to share stories about his childhood, and was a great source of advice. Tony was the one who tossed around a football with Troy in his backyard after school. Tony was the one who encouraged Troy by going to his baseball games when my father did not. As a matter of fact, father was only motivated to go to Troy's baseball games because "Tony has been going." It wasn't out of genuine interest, but to save face in front of others. Tony referred to my brother as the son he never had, and Troy was more than thrilled to have Tony as a father figure.

My brother's relationship with our father was very poor. It would only make him angry when my father would put on a show for guests by affectionately referring to him as "my boy" or "my son." Keeping up appearances with other family members or the neighbors was more important to our parents than actually being genuinely caring to their own children.

Troy was also angered by my mother for her lack of involvement as a parent, or for vouching for him. She never attended any of his games because she "wasn't interested in those things." She provided him with the material necessities—clothes, food, etc.—but there was no emotional support when he was sad, or upset.

As he grew older, my brother was convinced that Mom would purposely try to push his buttons, just for the sake of making him angry. It irritated him that his own mother was unable to discern the various emotions of her own son, or worse, would consciously aggravate him. The emotional connection to our mother and father was feeble at best.

Despite this, during one of our discussions about our parents in which I informed Troy that our father would not be welcome in my future, just like Micah, he protested. Troy said that although our parents were not the best parents in the world, there were far worse out there. He reminded me that they chose to raise us.

He said, "It's not like they threw us in a dumpster when we were born."

He was right. There were worse parents out there. We had a roof over our heads, the house was warm on cold winter nights, we had food in our bellies, we lived in a safe district, and we received a great education. But is that where parenthood ends?

I sighed. "Troy, they didn't abort us as babies, but there are still things that they have done which are inexcusable."

Perplexed, Troy asked, "Why?"

I replied, "There are too many things, and it is too long of a story to tell." Then I changed the subject.

As a big sister, it has always been my role to protect my brother. No matter how big he got, he would always be my baby brother, although he constantly insists that I refer to him instead as my "younger" brother.

I clearly remember being rushed to my neighbor's house in the middle of the night when my mother's water broke and she went into labor. I was five years old and terrified as I looked outside the window, watching my father put my mom in the back seat of the car and drive away. My Portuguese neighbor tried to calm me by giving me chocolate milk, but I only wanted my comforting strawberry milk, which she didn't have. I must've stared out the window for half an hour until I was encouraged to go to sleep.

The next day, I went with my father to pick out "It's a Boy" balloons for my mom and the new baby. I was very anxious to make sure my mom was okay and to meet my new brother. My father held my hand as we walked into the hospital room. My mother was seated in the hospital bed, and Troy was sleeping in a little cubby next to her. I immediately ran to her and gave her a hug. I hadn't gotten any sleep the night before, and I was relieved to see her doing okay. The last time I had seen her, she had been screaming in pain. As she lay in the hospital bed, she was all smiles.

My father picked up the baby and held him in his arms. On my tiptoes, I peered over the blanket that enveloped him to see what he looked like. He looked at me with big, black, curious eyes. His hands were so tiny, and they were tightly clenched. I tried to open them, but his little fingers wrapped tightly around my one finger. I was intrigued by this little creature. I remember wondering why his skin wasn't brown like mine; he looked white. When my parents let me hold him for the first time, I remember feeling so terrified. "Watch his head, and hold his bottom," they said. He squirmed in my arms and cried as I held him awkwardly, unsure of what to do. I was officially a big sister from that moment on, and I knew that it was a big sister's job to look after her little brother.

As he grew older, he became my buddy and my partner in crime. We became very attached. We spent most of our time together. When I got the chicken pox, shortly after, he got it as well. If I got pink-eye, so did he. No matter how many times Mom told him to stay away from me, he stuck by my side, asking, "Cassandra, what's wrong with you?"

We'd ride our bikes up and down the block, me on my two-wheeler and him on his tricycle. We splashed together in the little plastic blow-up pool in Philadelphia, and later in the large in-ground pool in Edison. We played school: I was the teacher, and he was the student. I taught him how to recite his ABC's, how to spell his name, and how to write.

I didn't mind playing "boy" games with Troy as he grew older. When he wanted, we would toss a football back and forth in the back or kick around a soccer ball. When we were inside, we would run around the house playing the "gun game," like a version of tag where we would use our hands as guns and fake-shoot each other. (Father didn't approve of toy guns.) It was like they did in cowboy movies, crouching behind tables, and hiding around walls, trying to get the first shot. We played video-games together, and if I didn't feel like playing, I'd just watch. We shared a TV, and I had to put up with his lame wrestling shows, while he put up with my "lame girly shows."

As a teenager, he came to me for advice about girls, the changes that come with puberty, sex—the whole gamut. Although at times it was uncomfortable hearing things that an older sister doesn't want to hear coming from her baby brother, I had to handle it. I wanted to be there for him and always be the person he could talk to. It wasn't like he would speak to my parents about such things.

Of course, like typical siblings, we would fight, but in the end, we always looked out for one another. Without my brother in my life, I'm not sure what kind of person I would be today. In a home in which my parents were both distant, we were each other's only source of attention, comfort, and support. The only other person who provided that for me was my grandmother for a few months out of the year. My brother was my best friend, and without him, I may not have the warmth in my heart that I do today.

I struggled with my decision to tell my brother about what had happened to me. I was the older sister, which meant that my burdens should not be his. Nonetheless, as I'd felt that it would've been a betrayal in not telling him about my adoption, I felt the same way about not telling him about my sexual abuse. He had to hear about it before my mother did; he couldn't hear it from anyone else but me. We were not only siblings, we were best friends.

I worried about how he would react. Maybe he wouldn't be able to handle it because Dad was his biological father. He had Dad's blood coursing through his veins. Would that affect the way he would view himself? What about the way that he would view me? I knew that he wouldn't judge me, like I feared others would. But I knew he would have many questions that I wouldn't want to answer. Perhaps he was too young to understand. I wanted to protect him from the ugliness of the world, and of his own father. What if he just couldn't contain himself the way that I had been able to for so many years? What if my story would be the final straw for him, causing him to go ballistic? What if he just punched my father, square in the face, causing chaos in the home before my carefully scheduled disclosure? The many possibilities raced through my mind.

As Troy got older, although my role didn't change towards him, his did towards me. I was still the protective older sister, but he took on the role as the protective younger brother. His voice grew deeper, and there was no longer any confusion when someone called the house phone whether it was he or I who had answered. He towered over me and had muscles that were apparent through his clothes. My baby brother had become a man. It became his job to protect and defend me. Maybe it would be better if he didn't know. That way he could continue to function in the house, with a roof over his head, and focus on more important things like school.

Troy pressed me about what experiences I had with our parents that made me feel so different. He knew me well, and he knew that I was holding something back from him since that conversation we had about our non-aborting parents.

"Troy, I don't know if you are ready to handle what I have to tell you."

"You said the same thing about telling me that you're my half-sister too, but I handled it."

I cringed, "Yeah, but you *actually* called me your half-sister!"

"Yeah, for all of two minutes. I'm a lot more mature now. Can't you see in the past year how much I've changed?"

He had changed. He had become more responsible and more thoughtful with his actions. "Yeah, but this is about your parents...I don't know how you will take it."

"Listen, if Dad shot a man, whether he's my father or not, he is still guilty of shooting a man. It doesn't make a difference to me."

"Troy, you have to live here. You have to sleep in a room right next to theirs. I don't know if you can do that knowing all of the things they've done to wrong me."

Adamantly, he insisted, "Cassandra, you know I barely see them or talk to them already. It won't make a difference."

I knew that by telling my brother about what happened to me, I wouldn't be destroying a great relationship. Yet, I knew that something so serious *would* make a difference. "I'll tell you when I'm ready."

Troy gave me a sideways look, as if he suspected that I did not intend to tell him at all. "Okay," he said, "I'll be waiting."

A couple of days later, while my brother and I sat and talked in the living room, I brought up Mr. D. We discussed how Troy had been so young that he had no idea what was going on. We speculated who the mysterious adult was that I told. I brought up how gross he was with his tobacco stains.

Then I strategically asked, "Hey, what if Mr. D was your father? What would you do?" I tried to be casual about it.

Troy looked at me awkwardly, as if he didn't want to entertain the idea, and said, "I don't know."

I kept my gaze on him, looking for more of a response: verbal or physical.

He gave me a blank stare. He deflected the question as soon as it came to him, not giving it a chance to digest.

I let it be and moved on.

I knew I had to tell my brother but I didn't know when. The next day, I decided that I needed to make a timeline. Once I disclosed my abuse, there would be a domino effect of repercussions. It was May, and I didn't want to miss my brother's nineteenth birthday, so I planned to leave immediately afterwards in mid-August.

I decided that it would be fair to my mother if I at least stayed in the area for one month after disclosing the abuse, so that if she did want to reach out and communicate with me, I would be readily available to her. I knew that she had to overcome the initial shock, and one month was ample time for her to receive any clarification she needed and for her to say whatever she needed to say to me in person. During that month's time, I would stay at a friend's home as a transition before the final move to Georgia. I decided that the best day to tell her would be a Friday, because she works during the day on Fridays. That would give me all day to pack up all of my belongings into my car. When she returned from work, I would be ready and waiting for her.

I picked a date: July 8th. I labeled it Doomsday, or D-Day. It was set, marked on my calendar. I would sit with her outside, and tell her everything. I would return the house key and inform her that I would be moving to Georgia, and that I would be in the area for exactly one month.

I had not yet decided what it would mean if she didn't contact me before I moved to Georgia. I thought it would be hard, knowing that I waited for her for one month and that she didn't reach out to me. It would make the door of communication that much harder to open if she decided to approach me at a later date.

The one-month grace period was not just for my mother; it was for me, too. It was for me to work through my thoughts and feelings with Teti. Since I had no clue how my mother would take the news, I couldn't fathom my own reaction. So meeting with Teti after the disclosure was crucial.

I also wanted to spend time with my friends. During two years of graduate school, I had gone out only on a handful of occasions, which tended to be just birthdays. Since my graduation and my unemployment, I was absolutely freed of any obligations, which made me much more available to be the social person that I truly was. I was speaking to friends much more frequently, seeing them more often, and actually having the time to enjoy friendships like they should be enjoyed.

It was bittersweet. I was happy that I was rekindling my friendships, yet it would be short-lived since I would be moving soon. There were classmates who had turned into friends, and I had just started to get to know them outside of school. I had started to feel the nostalgia before I had gone away.

Most importantly, that grace period was for my brother. We had also been spending more time together. Our relationship reset to how it was before I went away to college. We woke up early every morning and went to run on the local high school's track. We spent our days together playing video games, going to basketball games, and just hanging out. I didn't want to leave so abruptly, as our relationship got to be so good.

Furthermore, he needed time to process the information I was about to tell him. I knew that as a man, he wouldn't be quick to express the emotions that he would feel upon my disclosure. He would consider that as being "weak" and not "manly." He deserved more time than my mother, and I was sure that he would need more time than she did.

I decided that I would tell Troy a month and a half before I told my mother. I hoped that he would come to me during that time period to express himself. I would offer to sit and talk with him, and even that he come with me to see Teti to get things off of his chest and process his emotions. It's not every day that a person is told that his father is a pedophile. It was not only important that he process it before my disclosure to my mother but after the disclosure as well. Not knowing how my mom would take it, I wasn't sure how it would affect him. How was he to respond if my mother were to slap me in the face and tell me that she didn't believe me? How was he to live in the house with parents who had hurt his sister who he cares about so deeply?

With that thought, I realized that it suddenly became urgent for me to tell him. I had been so focused on my plans that I didn't realize that my brother might have to make plans of his own. On May 18th, fifty-one days before the newly scheduled D-day, I called my brother into my room and asked him to sit down.

He sat on my bed attentively. He knew I was ready to disclose what I had been holding back from him.

I sat there, in my pajamas, unsure of what to say. My heart trilled in my chest, and my armpits were moist with perspiration.

15

"What did they do to you?" Troy started, getting to business.

I pursed my lips. I took a deep breath and asked him, "What is the worst thing that a father could do to a daughter?"

He looked away and after a brief pause said, "Well—I mean—there are some things, but I don't even want to go in that direction." He moved his hand, as if to push away the thought.

I looked at him, biting the inside of my cheek, and urged, "No, go in that direction."

His jaw clenched and his body became tense.

I held my breath and waited for him to speak.

"Did he penetrate you?" he asked.

I was aghast. I didn't expect such extreme bluntness at all. I replied, "I don't think that's impor—"

"No," he interrupted, "Did he penetrate you?" He stared unwaveringly at an invisible spot on the wall before him.

"Yes," I answered dutifully.

Troy had taken complete control of this discussion. He wasn't letting me shield him from the ugly. He wanted the full un-sugar-coated truth, head-on.

I noticed Troy's hand ball up into a fist. "Did he finish inside you?" he asked in a slightly strained voice.

"No," I answered. Uncomfortable and panicked at my lack of control in this conversation, I said, "Listen, we're not going through every single detail of what happened."

He acquiesced. I could see that he was deep in thought as he stared at the wall. Although I had regained control, I was so rattled that I didn't know how to continue. I just stared, trying to see the spot he was focused so intently on.

He finally turned to look at me, "When did it stop?"

"When I was fourteen."

He did the math in his head. He mumbled to himself, "I was nine, so I couldn't have done anything."

"What do you mean?" I asked.

"I was thinking if I could've protected you."

"You couldn't have done anything, Troy." I tried to reassure him. "You can't blame yourself; do you hear me?"

He nodded. After some silence, he said, "I know."

"I actually thought Mom did the same thing to you at first," I followed up.

He looked at me, perplexed.

I explained, "He started when I was five or six. He told me that those were things that a father should do. And once Mom found my bra in their bedroom, I thought she did the same things to you. I felt that it was wrong but I didn't say or do anything..."

"What were you supposed to do, Cassandra? You were a kid. Maybe if I was older than you, you could've told me. But you didn't have anybody to tell."

"Yeah, but I wish I could've stopped it."

"Come on. You can't blame yourself. He's the one who took advantage of you." Here was my little brother playing the role of protective big brother.

"I just wish that someone—anyone—would have told me otherwise. We didn't even have 'the sex talk.'"

"Well, you gotta remember where they come from. They're Haitian, not American. They don't talk about that stuff. Remember, *you're* the one who gave me my sex talk."

He was right; I was the one who gave him the sex talk, among countless other lessons. We sat in silence. I was thinking about how maturely Troy was handling this. I looked over at him, and he resumed his icy stare at the wall, his body tense and his jaw line defined.

He broke the silence, "You know Mom is not going to leave him right?"

"Truthfully, I don't have much faith that she will."

"Well, you know that Haitians don't get divorced," he reasoned.

"That's true."

I was reminded of my mother's cousin who continued to stay with her verbally abusive and cheating husband. My grandmother stayed with my grandfather who had a child with another woman while they were still married.

Shaking my head, I insisted, "But I can't imagine a person making the choice to continue to stay with the person who took advantage of their daughter. That's just crazy!"

Troy shrugged, "Who knows. She's old. Dad puts up with her stuff. It may just be the easier choice to not believe you."

I let out a sigh. "When I was little I used to look up to her for always talking about handling her own business, and being independent, but she literally has nothing in her name. Everything is under Dad's control, which is so frustrating, especially in a situation like this."

Troy shrugged again. "How are you able to look him in the face every day and have a conversation with him?" The wheels had been turning in his head and he looked confounded.

"When you do it for years, you get used to it," I shrugged. "Also, it wasn't something that was really on my mind until I started working with Teti. So there have been countless times when I wanted to gut him with a knife, trust me. I just got really good at holding things in."

We sat again in silence, while Troy was deep in thought. I was patient with him, looking for any signs of change in his nonverbal cues.

I asked, "How does it feel to hear all of this?" I put my big sister and therapist hat on.

"Well, I understand why you hate Dad so much. It makes more sense why you decided to move to Georgia."

"Well, it's not the only reason I'm moving."

"True, but it's a part of it. You should tell Micah about it since you plan on living with him, and this is a guy who you're serious about."

"You're right." Again, I was surprised at his maturity.

"I feel like there are so many secrets in this house. Two years ago it was the adoption. Now it's this."

That was his way of finally revealing how he was feeling inside. It was cryptic, but it was Troy. I understood that at that moment he was overwhelmed, and I felt for him. I felt guilty for being the constant bearer of bad news. With each piece of information I brought forward, the less trust he had for our parents. I didn't know what to say.

After some time, I asked, "What are you going to do?" I wanted to know how he planned on coping with this new information.

"I guess I'll do what you did and just stick it out until I can join the police academy."

I wasn't sure how realistic that would be, knowing Troy's already unsteady relationship with Pierre, but I decided to give him some time to process this information. I knew that he was going to need to digest what he had just heard. I asked, "Do you want to go to Teti with me? I'm going to see her tomorrow."

"Nah. There's nothing to tell her," he shrugged.

"Tell her how you feel, Troy." Inside I was pleading for him to go. I desperately wanted him to talk about the confusing emotions he was feeling inside, especially before my move.

"I don't know her. You have a relationship with her, and I don't, so I don't think I'm going."

I wasn't surprised by his answer, but I didn't think it would hurt to ask anyway.

After that conversation, I made sure to check on him regularly, and to be particularly observant of any changes in mood. I would ask, "How do you feel about the situation?" or "What do you plan on doing?" and "Do you think you'll be okay?"

Troy insisted that he was fine and told me to stop probing his brain. He informed me that he had no problem avoiding our parents. He decided that he could busy himself for a whole day at school, from going to class, going to the gym, and hanging out with friends. He said that he had to stay in the house because Mom and Dad were helping him with school and he didn't want to take out any loans and graduate with too much debt.

Knowing Troy's close relationship with me, and his already existent anger towards Pierre, I knew that it was only matter of time and the right amount of pushed buttons for Troy to explode. I urged him to reconsider, normalizing debt as something as common to the everyday American as a cell phone. He only had a part-time job and didn't have the funds to live on his own. He briefly mentioned the Army as a final resort, but I told him that was not an option at all. In times like this—where being deployed is very much a reality—I couldn't bear the idea of my brother jumping out of the frying pan into the fire. I didn't know how to get him out of that house, and Troy didn't seem optimistic about even looking at options for getting out. On the surface, he appeared as peaceful as a placid pond. But beneath, his waters were turbulent and thunderous. He just didn't know it yet.

⌒⟨⟩⌒

Within a few weeks, things finally boiled over. Prior to my disclosure to Troy, all interactions between my brother and father were minimal and brief. After the disclosure, the frequency and length of encounters hadn't changed, but Troy's tolerance for him wore very thin. Father seemed to be bugging him about everything, and tensions were rising. It reached a point where finally our father had antagonized Troy one too many times.

It was Father's Day, and Father was in a bad mood because he had not received a card from either of us. He jumped at the opportunity to play victim.

"What have I possibly done to you guys to deserve this treatment? As my children, I have done nothing but love you and provide for you. Where did I go wrong as a father that I deserve this mistreatment?" he said, of course, within earshot of my mother, who then, with sadness in her eyes, echoed what Father said, personally hurt that we were so mean to him.

"You know your father is a sensitive man."

I can't speak for Troy, but it made my blood boil. What settled me down was knowing that I would be leaving in only a few weeks, and I would never have to look at his face again. It was the only fact that put me in a state of calm. In the meantime, I decided to go out to the movies to get away.

Later that day, while I was out, whether it was out of being petty or because of his need to assert his authority, he insisted that my brother disclose the contents of his mail. When Troy declined to do so, not to be undermined, Father became verbally aggressive, screaming inches away from Troy's face, provoking Troy to in turn raise his voice. Pierre was not accustomed to anyone, let alone a "child" yelling at him, for any reason.

Pierre informed my brother that since it was his house, he had the right to inquire about or open any and all mail that came to the house. He was marking his territory and asserting himself as the Alpha male.

Troy did not back down this time. He told Pierre that unless he placed the order for the package himself and purchased it with his own money, he didn't need to know the contents of Troy's mail.

Pierre retaliated with his usual threat, "Do you want me to hit you?"

Typically, Troy would appease him by saying "No," and Pierre would get the last words by saying, "Well then, you'd better shape up." It would stroke Pierre's ego, confirming his status as king of his castle. This time, however, was different.

Troy firmly planted his feet, his broad shoulders taking up most of the hallway, eyes unwaveringly fixed on Pierre's, and said in a deep, quiet voice, "Go right ahead."

Pierre's eyes widened in shock. This was not how the script was supposed to go. He balled his hand into a fist and propelled it towards the center of Troy's chest. Troy was far more agile and quickly defended himself by placing his hands on Pierre's shoulders and pushing him away. Pierre surged forward once more and threw several punches at Troy, but all were futile. Troy easily dodged each and every one of his attempts. Pierre struggled to catch his breath. He was flustered; it was evident who had won this battle.

Infuriated by his inability to inflict physical pain on Troy, Pierre threatened to tell Tony, our neighbor, that Troy had attacked him. Pierre knew that Troy had a good relationship with Tony. He probably knew that Troy was closer to Tony than he was, and he jumped at the opportunity to play victim and attack Troy emotionally by defaming his character to Tony. Troy was already seeing red, but with the threat of telling Tony, he was steaming. He turned his back and walked back into his room, suppressing the urge to teach Pierre the difference between a push and an "attack." He knew that Pierre was weak and that it wasn't worth it. But he also knew that something had to change.

The fuse had been lit, and Troy had turned into a ticking time bomb. It suddenly became urgent for him to find a way to get out of the house. Just getting by, as he had previously suggested, was no longer an option.

Troy desperately needed to speak with someone about what had happened, a voice of reason to calm him down. Since I was unavailable, he called his good friend Ronny, who came over without question. They talked for hours, and he told him everything, from the endless conflict he had with Pierre throughout childhood to my sexual abuse. Ronny sat, absorbing the information that Troy placed before him.

After a long and deep silence, Ronny offered that Troy stay at his parents' home. Troy was grateful for his unexpected offer, as Ronny's family had already viewed Troy as a family member, but he would have to wait on the official answer from Ronny's parents.

The anger towards Pierre continued to boil inside of Troy, but he felt some relief, being able to confide in a close friend about what he was going through. Troy did not see or speak to Pierre for the entire week.

The next weekend, Troy noticed Pierre speaking to Tony and his wife outside. He observed his facial expressions and mannerisms from my bedroom window. He was immediately infuriated, convinced that Pierre was vilifying him. To keep the peace, I tried to convince Troy that it had most likely been an empty threat and that Pierre wouldn't have involved Tony in family drama. Troy was fuming, and I was panicked.

It was only a few weeks until D-Day and I wanted very much to keep the lid on things. Unfortunately, it was a matter that was no longer in my hands. This was no longer my personal struggle. It was now Troy's issue as well.

The next day, Tony was seated on his front stoop, smoking a cigarette while Troy pulled in the driveway, coming from work. As usual, Troy walked over to say hello. Meanwhile, I anxiously looked outside my bedroom window, wondering what was going to happen. They started talking, and then stepped out of my line of sight.

Throughout the day, Troy had been texting me while he was at work, describing how he was convinced that Pierre was trying to ruin his image to Tony. He called me during his lunch break, enraged, disowning Mom for not vouching for him in the argument with Pierre. Apparently after the altercation with Pierre, Mom had gone into his room, and instead of asking what happened, she stated, "I can't believe that you would even think to raise your hand at your father." He ranted about many examples in his childhood in which Mom did not take his side or support him. The only stance she stood for was alongside Pierre. Battling with my own struggle with Mom, I was devoid of words to calm him and could only listen.

As Troy approached Tony, the first words out of Tony's mouth were "Troy, why are you being disrespectful to your father, huh?"

To Troy, those words confirmed what a low-life animal Pierre was. He didn't deserve the legs that allowed him to walk amongst civilized people. Instead, he deserved to crawl on his belly, like the manipulative and conniving snake that he was.

Troy replied, "Tony, I apologize on behalf of my father for coming here and involving you with this, and I apologize in advance for having to explain my side of the story."

16

"What happened?" I asked as Troy walked into my room.

He shut the door behind him, and with a shrug he said, "I told you that Pierre told Tony."

My heart stumbled like a bad drummer. Not wanting to know the answer, I asked, "What did you say to Tony?"

He looked me in the eyes and replied, "I told him the truth."

"Damn, damn, damn," I said to myself, "Shit, this is getting out of control... Now Tony knows?" My story, which I had contained for over a decade, had sprung a leak and was spilling fast.

"Yup," Troy said matter-of-factly. He continued, "I couldn't have him going around, painting me black, especially to a person like Tony, who I respect."

I shook my head in silence, imagining the water trickling from our home, oozing onto Tony's perfect green lawn. Troy had always been more ballsy than I was. I sat back for years while my father portrayed me as a horrible person—and while he played the role of an innocent victim to my mother. On the other hand, after I unveiled Pierre's true ugly character, Troy became intolerant of any defamation of his integrity. I sat on my bed, thinking that with this news, Tony's world had been polluted.

Tony's idea of the perfect neighborhood—with his friendly neighbor whose garbage can he would always pull from the curb if forgotten, his neighbor with whom he'd share his tools, his neighbor with whom he would chat regularly—was completely polluted. I felt immediate guilt. Nobody wants their perfect world to be contaminated, and the muckiness of my life, which I kept bottled up and hidden, was seeping into other people's lives. It my muckiness, and I felt fully responsible.

I felt the same way about disclosing to my close friend, Brianna. In a discussion about moving to Georgia, Brianna questioned the urgency for me to get out of my home. She didn't like the idea of me moving so far away from her and wasn't fond of the idea of me making such a big move to be with my boyfriend. To her, it was more logical to move for a job opportunity, or to be with family. I knew no one in Georgia, and she was understandably worried.

I had always been the risk-taker in our relationship of six years. I ventured alone to Spain to study abroad. I took the risk of running my own business in a foreign town in South Jersey where I had to sleep in my office because I had neither a place to live nor a car to drive. I was the one to get piercings on impulse. And now, I was the one who made the decision to move over eight-hundred miles away to pursue love. To her, it was probably the biggest risk of all that I was taking.

Once I had turned eighteen, I endlessly sought ways to get as far away from my parents as possible. Rutgers University was literally fifteen minutes from my house, and although I attended because I received a full academic scholarship, I made certain that I would be living on campus, away from my parents.

Brianna, on the other hand, had a very close relationship with her parents and although she attended college in another state, she could never imagine herself moving hundreds of miles away from them. She had also found herself in the role of caretaker in her parent's old age, causing the link between her and her parents to be even more tethered. Based on her own loving and close relationship with her parents, she insisted that my parents loved me and that they were simply poor at expressing their love.

At that point, Brianna had known me for six years and was well aware of the poor relationship I had with my parents. Yet the ideal "mom equals love" equation surpassed the concrete examples of wrongdoing on her part. What she saw was the warm, welcoming mother who was kind to her whenever she visited my home. Those moments held much more weight than any amount of transgressions.

Out of frustration at the unfounded idealization of my mother, I informed her quite extemporaneously about the sexual abuse. Initially, she seemed to have taken it well, until one day she informed me that the disclosure of my sexual abuse had begun to interfere with her daily life.

I had felt relieved to tell her about what I was going through, because as my closest friend, she now knew all aspects of me, good and ugly. Now she knew the ugliest part of me. I had become comfortable in discussing with her my struggles and decisions I had to make related to disclosing to my family and to moving. Yet, I was so engrossed in what was going on with me that I failed to realize how my situation was affecting Brianna.

Brianna shared with me her continual sense of discomfort; my sexual abuse became something that was on her mind every day, causing her to feel helpless. This was not a situation in which she could simply take clothes out of a closet and throw out the offender. She was filled with fear that after my disclosure, I would be unequipped to handle the consequences, turn into a different person, maybe even go crazy. It had become evident that my muckiness had invaded her life, and she felt overwhelmed. I felt immense guilt, doubting my role as a good friend by inadvertently placing my burdens on her. I felt responsible for her discomfort.

After becoming aware of the spread of my muckiness to others, I sincerely struggled with my instinct to withdraw. As I had always done before, I wanted to bury the ugly parts of my life to ensure the comfort of those around me. A battle waged on inside of me with one nagging question: *should I trudge forward?* Planning to tell about my sexual abuse and planning to move to a new state at the same time made me feel like my world was upside down. So much was happening in a short period of time. I had lost my job. I would soon be graduating from school and taking my licensing exam. I was preparing for my disclosure to my mother, trying to spend quality time with my friends, and getting ready to move to Georgia. I struggled with serious anxiety. I was on edge almost all of the time and was prone to mood swings. Any additional stressor, no matter how small, produced high-strung reactions.

Luckily, Brianna kindly offered to let me stay at her parents' house during the one-month grace period after my disclosure to Mom. She wanted to make sure I had the chance to reconcile with my mother, and she was especially concerned that I would have the opportunity to work things out with my therapist. It was her way of providing me with support; it was my motivation to push forward. Furthermore, we could spend some more time together before my move. There had been a great decrease in the frequency of our visits. We went from being roommates, and seeing each other every day, to seeing each other perhaps once per month due to graduate school. Knowing that I would be able to stay with her was a relief. It was one less thing I had to worry about, but I still couldn't escape the sharp unease deep within my chest.

Teti informed me that one of the most stressful things to occur in a person's life is moving alone. No wonder my nerves were a wreck. The thought of moving to a southern state was scary, yet simultaneously exciting. Atlanta wasn't going to be like the bustling New York City, but in Atlanta, I saw a future with a man I loved. The yearlong long distance relationship had taken its toll on me, and either Micah had to move to New Jersey, or I had to move to Georgia.

Perks for Georgia included: Warmer weather, mild winters, and cheap real estate, closer to Florida for vacation. Perks for Jersey included: Closer to friends, closer to Troy, enjoyment of NYC thrills, and the comfort of my familiar surroundings and family. I had to remind myself of my reasons, and reassure myself that I was making the right decision. In the end, Micah had a stable job and a cheap apartment and I had neither; by spending a few years in Georgia, we would be able to save up money for our wedding and our future.

Both of us were taking a huge step by choosing to live together. There was so much to be considered. I had already gotten past my initial struggles to let Micah into my heart, and now he would be welcoming me into his home. I was fearful of what it would be like to live with him; having seen his dreadfully messy apartment in college, I had reason to be afraid. But aside from cleanliness, I was worried about getting used to waking up next to him every single morning. As much as I knew that I was madly in love with him, there was something scary about that thought. What if I got annoyed at seeing his face every day? What if we got into an argument? Where could I go to escape? And what if he grew tired of me? It was certainly a risk.

Even while I was packing my belongings, I was laden with sorrow. I packed all of my memories into brown cardboard boxes. As heavy as the boxes were, they weren't nearly as heavy as my heart. I realized that I may never return to this house or call it home ever again. I packed my baby photo albums, my baby stuffed animals, my sculpture of my hand from kindergarten, my awards from middle school, my communion dress, and my prom dress. I didn't want to leave anything behind.

As I packed, I daydreamed about what a "regular" move-out would have been like. I imagined my mother helping me pack my things, making sure I had everything I needed. I saw myself visiting the family with my husband in the future and staying in my room, which would be exactly the way that I left it, complete with the stuffed animals on my bed and high school pictures on the wall. During my visits, we would sit in the garage, go through a box of childhood things and laugh at the awkward pictures of me while my mother told embarrassing stories to my husband about when I was younger.

Apparently I had watched too many episodes of *The Cosby Show*, because such was not my life. I checked different corners of the house over and over again; I couldn't afford to leave any precious memories behind.

17

I n addition to my material belongings, I also had to find a
way to hold onto my family. Although my immediate family
is small, my extended family is huge. My grandmother is
one of, no exaggeration, about fifty brothers and sisters. That
means lots and lots of cousins, half of whom I have yet to meet.
But even the ones that I knew of were only seen during parties
or rare barbeques, perhaps twice per year, and the relationships weren't close.

My parents were isolated in central Jersey and most of my
family lived in New York. I remember far more frequent interactions with my cousins when I was younger, when we would
have regular visits "just because." But as I grew older, my parents no longer visited family for fun and became more consistent in declining invitations to celebrate birthdays, graduations,
and even funerals from family members. The common excuse
was that they were working or tired from work. My cousins,
who were initially close, quickly became like strangers. I decided that it was imperative for me to host a graduation party.

Although I did indeed want to celebrate my last graduation
from school ever—I did not intend to ever return to school after
those grueling two years—the "graduation" party had so many

ulterior motives. I wanted it to be an opportunity for my extended family to meet Micah, who would be in attendance. I figured that the next time that they would see him would be at the altar for our wedding. It was also an opportunity for me to spend time with my family prior to my move and, most crucially, to get contact information from them so that I wouldn't have to rely on my parents as a link to the rest of my family.

I had no idea what would happen after the disclosure. My mom might shun me, and then I would be left without any connection to them. I wasn't sure whether news of the disclosure would even reach them, knowing how private a person my mother is, but I still wanted to have the option to contact them, knowing that they most likely didn't have a way to directly contact me.

My mother, although unenthused and resistant about the responsibility of hosting a party, went to work on inviting family members and getting party supplies. I purchased a notebook to record all addresses, found a DJ, and invited friends. I felt excited at being able to party with my family and friends, but saddened because only two weeks after the party was the scheduled D-day. I had to savor the family time.

Due to travel expenses, and since Micah was travelling all the way to New York specifically to attend my graduation celebration, I asked my mother if she'd mind Micah staying with us at the house. Obviously, since he and I weren't married, he wouldn't be staying in my room, and I suggested that he stay downstairs. After a few days of uncertainty and constant reminding from me, she said yes, he could stay in the downstairs room. I was happy to tell him the news—hotel expenses are not cheap!

I prepared the room for him so that he would have a comfortable stay. I spent hours doing laundry, washing sheets, comforters, and pillow-cases, dragging an extra mattress from the other room to make his night on the hard pull-out sofa more comfortable.

The night he was due to arrive, there were severe weather conditions, and his flight was continually delayed hour by hour. I waited in my room, lying on my bed fully dressed for his flight to depart from Atlanta.

As I waited, watching whatever was on TV, I heard a car pull up, a quick knock on the door, and then a car driving away. It was about 10 p.m.; who could be coming over at this time? I went out of my room to discover my twelve-year-old cousin downstairs.

"What are you doing here?" I asked.

In her tiny voice, she looked at me, shrugged her shoulders, and said in her thick Haitian accent, "I don't know."

"Are you spending the night?"

"Yes," she responded as if she was unsure if her answer was correct. I noticed she had a bag with pajamas and a toothbrush.

"But where is your brother, Krystall and Jacqueline? They usually come with you."

Again, she shrugged with a nervous smile, "I don't know."

My suspicions increased. "What reason did your mom tell you to come over tonight?

"I don't know. She just said, 'You're going to Cassandra's house tonight.'"

As a person who doesn't believe in coincidences, I asked for further clarification, "She specifically said Cassandra's house? Not Troy's house? Or Aunty or Uncle's house?"

"Yes," she replied, "She said Cassandra's house."

Already annoyed at Micah's delayed flight, I felt my blood pressure rising. I needed a second opinion. I had a theory brewing but I didn't want to jump to conclusions. I went to Troy's room and informed him of the situation.

He looked at it logically and figured that she was probably over because they didn't have enough room for the whole family in the van for the party, which was the next day. Troy followed me downstairs and we continued the interrogation.

"You have to know something. Did your mom talk to our mom on the phone?" Troy inquired.

"Yes," her nervous smile returned. Now she had two people staring intently at her.

"What were they saying?" he asked.

"I don't know," she said.

"Come on, you really know nothing?" I asked, giving her a playful look, indicating that I knew that she knew why she was there.

"I swear, I don't know."

I started to feel bad. This girl was innocent. She, like an obedient Haitian child, simply followed orders without question and just so happened to end up in my house, by herself, watching TV on the couch. She didn't even know where she was supposed to sleep.

Finally, I asked, "Marie, how many people do you have in your family?"

"Six."

Troy followed up, "And how many people can fit in your van?"

"Seven."

Troy and I looked at each other. That's all we needed to know. We had ruled out the possibility that she needed to spend the night for transportation to the party. Her family's van could fit them all. And there was no other purpose of her being at my house, all alone, dropped off at 10 o'clock at night, on the same day Micah was scheduled to arrive.

My initial hypothesis was correct: Marie had evidently been sent as a chaperone. Typically people think that chaperones are supervisory adults who are responsible for the welfare of children, but not to my parents. Maybe it was a Haitian thing, or maybe it was specific to how my parents handled things. I wasn't unfamiliar with this situation.

When I was in high school, if I had a male classmate come over to my house to work on a project, my little brother would coincidentally always be in the room. I remember asking him once what he was doing hanging around while my classmate and I did schoolwork. And very much like Marie, he responded,

"I don't know. Mom and Dad told me to stay down here until you are done with your project." He clearly wasn't happy being forced to stay in the room with me. He would rather be outside or in his room playing. It wasn't even as if my classmate and I were in my bedroom. We were in the den, an open room downstairs. It mildly annoyed me then, when I was fifteen; it infuriated me now that I was twenty-five.

Growing up in the Haitian culture, I was very familiar with the double standard for men and women. I wasn't allowed to so much as look at a boy until I was completely finished with school, but immediately after, I was expected to be married and reproducing. Micah was the only boyfriend I introduced to my parents, and he was the man who I was planning on marrying. I knew better than to introduce anyone else because I'd most likely be considered a *jeness* as my mother casually referred to many girls.

As soon as my brother hit puberty, both of my parents would joke about how many girls he would conquer and chase. They explained to me that if I went out and got pregnant, I would be the one bringing the baby home to have to take care of, whereas if Troy got somebody pregnant, he didn't have to bring the baby home. It was evident that throughout the years, the double standard persisted. My brother, at age nineteen, had a girlfriend who frequented the house and spent endless hours behind closed doors in his room unquestioned by my parents. I, at age twenty-five, asked permission for my boyfriend to spend the night downstairs and, without warning, was presented with a chaperone.

Aside from my anger, numerous things went through my mind. First, I was appalled that the double standard was clearly still in place and I was being treated like a child.

Secondly, the sneakiness of it all was incredibly immature and sophomoric. I lost respect for my mother, who couldn't look me in my face woman-to-woman and straightforwardly tell me that she didn't want Micah to spend the night in her home. Instead, she deviously arranged for my twelve-year-old cousin to be present as a chaperone, as if I wouldn't notice.

Thirdly, I started to wonder about how much respect I had for Marie's mom, who dropped her daughter off at my house without warning, with full awareness that she was to play the role of chaperone. Naturally, I would be sleeping upstairs in my bedroom, which meant that twelve-year-old Marie would be sleeping on the same floor as Micah, a man whom she had only heard of but never met in person. Where was her responsibility in protecting her daughter? For all she knew, Micah could've been a raging pedophile and Marie would've been a sitting duck, right into a potential predator's arms.

And lastly, what infuriated me the most and got me boiling-mad was that all of this idiotic planning had no one's safety in mind, not mine, and not Marie's.

Mother found it necessary to sneakily find me a chaperone for my boyfriend at twenty-five, yet did not find it necessary to take any precautions when I was left alone with a stranger at age five.

When Micah eventually arrived, he stayed at a hotel. He certainly didn't feel comfortable about the situation at all. When mother asked why he didn't spend the night, I explained, "Why would he, a grown man, want to share a space with a twelve-year-old girl?"

She didn't respond, her face was blank—she really didn't get it.

JUNE 18TH 2011 (D-DAY MINUS 20)

My father's sister, Tati Martha, had prepared most of the food, so my parents drove to Brooklyn early to help get things prepared. My mother's cousin, Tati Yvette, was hosting the party in her back yard in Queens. In Edison, New Jersey, Micah and I prepared ourselves for his introduction to my extended family.

Haitians are known to be very critical of non-Haitian newcomers, as is common with many immigrant families, so

I wanted to make sure that everything was perfect. We even made a last-minute outfit change, when Troy pointed out that Micah shouldn't make his appearance wearing shorts, even though it was a back yard party. I had overlooked that detail. Haitian males are known to arrive at barbeques in a button-up t-shirt, slacks and dress shoes. It was a Haitian thing.

On the way to the party, I gave him a few quick lessons: "Tati" means aunt, but not everyone called "tati" is an aunt. It's a term used for respect. The women will likely lean in for a hug and a kiss, so don't be startled. The men will be expecting a firm handshake. Don't be nervous about dancing to kompa music; they'll appreciate you just trying. And be prepared to answer a lot of questions. When we arrived at the party, Micah quickly acquainted himself with my family as he was put right to work, helping move tables and carry heavy cases of soda and beer.

As more people started to arrive, the energy started to pick up. Hugs and kisses were being exchanged exponentially and endless introductions were being made. There was a buzz of people talking and laughing, with the sound of children running around and having fun. I videotaped friends and family attempting to dance to the cha-cha slide. I looked over in the crowd and saw my aunts, uncles, and cousins having fun laughing and dancing with the family. It brought a smile to my face.

This is what I really loved: having a good time with family and friends. It was something that did not happen often enough. In my mind, I dreamed that this would be how my kids would grow up, surrounded by Micah's family and my family, having fun, laughing and celebrating each other. My family was able to have pure fun—no intoxication necessary.

The food was delectable. My Tati Martha completely outdid herself, providing three different kinds of rice, various types of meats and fish, and casseroles. There was so much food that people had Styrofoam plates loaded with food to take home. She also surprised me with a beautiful and delicious cake! I felt so flattered that she would do so much for me even though she wasn't even able to attend the celebration. As the owner of a catering company, she was incredibly busy, yet took her time and energy to cook such a variety of delicious dishes.

I felt so much appreciation and gratitude, and my heart filled with the happiness I felt, knowing that my family was supportive of me. Even though I didn't see them or speak to them often, they all came together on my behalf to celebrate my small victory.

I sat and smiled to myself, gazing out at my family. I felt the bass of the music thumping through my body. My taste buds were delighted by the delectable food. There was a warm glow in the backyard, as the daylight faded, and the fire torches illuminated the laughter and movements of the celebration. You could see the glistening sweat on people's foreheads as they danced. Everything was good. Micah brought me out of my deep thought, asking, "Can your aunt cook for our wedding? This food is delicious."

My smile faded. A little more than two weeks from that party, the whole dynamic of my family would change; just twenty days from that date was D-day. My loving aunt who had voluntarily cooked all of these delicious dishes, my aunt who was the hostess, my cousins, and my family members who were "not really family" could all potentially become my enemies.

It was a nice thought to think that at the wedding the reception would be just like this, but on a much larger scale. I imagined people giddy with happiness, showering Micah and I with love and gifts. If there was any party a Haitian enjoyed, it was a wedding reception. I imagined my aunts wanting to go dress shopping with me, volunteering to bake a towering white cake, chatting excitedly about marriage advice, and hopes of children. However, it was also a very realistic thought that much of my family might be absent not only at my wedding ceremony, but for the rest of my life. I spotted my mom dancing on the dance floor. It had been a very long time since I had seen her so full of energy and laughing the way she was.

I looked at Micah and with a pout, I signaled in her direction with my head, "She looks so happy; do I *have* to tell her the truth?" I wanted to stay in that moment of bliss forever.

He looked at me and shrugged, "It's up to you, Hun."

I wish he could've said, "No. You don't have to say anything, and everybody will continue to have fun and be happy together."

Too bad that's not how life worked. I knew I had to tell and I knew that it would continue to haunt me for the rest of my life if I didn't. But I couldn't let the future's uncertainty dampen my mood. I had this one night to spend time with family and friends, and I made it a point to enjoy it.

JUNE 19th 2011 (D-DAY MINUS 19)

The day following the graduation party, my father felt that it was his "fatherly duty" to have a "man-to-man" talk with Micah. Knowing the things my father did to me, it was difficult for Micah to contain himself, but he decided to mask his emotions—as I have done so many times in the past—so that he could get through the conversation.

Pierre sat with Micah outside on lawn chairs and spoke for over an hour.

First, he started to discuss landscaping, and how difficult it is to keep the lawn green. He followed up with expressing how annoying it is to have pesky groundhogs burrowing tunnels in the back yard.

Micah felt awkward, unsure how he should react to circumlocutory way of expression. He expected my father to be forward and straight to the point, clearly asking what his intentions were with me; yet, he waited patiently for him to get to the point.

Pierre went into a history lesson, discussing Haitian traditions with courtship, stating that a man interested in a woman should present a formal letter to her parents, expressing his value and requesting permission to date the woman. Furthermore, if he was to visit the woman's home, he was to sleep at the foot of the parent's bed.

After the history lesson, Pierre changed the topic to discuss how difficult it was to deal with Troy, and described him as lazy and unmotivated. He described how he tried hard as a parent to make him a good kid, but to no avail. He spoke of Troy as if he were a troubled and delinquent child, with an unpromising future.

Micah kept quiet and simply nodded. It was as if my father was looking for an ally in Micah, to rally with him against my brother. It only made Micah more uncomfortable, discussing Troy when he should have been discussing me.

After what seemed like an eternity, Pierre finally reached the point of the discussion, and asked what Micah's intentions were with me.

Micah informed him that he fully intended to marry me.

Father reacted by stating that things sometimes change and that although Micah may feel that he's in love, and that he may be excited, that situations and feelings may change. He then proceeded to go on a tangent about how he himself had gotten really hot and heavy with his previous girlfriends, and he thought that he was in love, but it was not the case.

Micah's discomfort grew even more. This was not the type of conversation he had anticipated. He became tense in his seat, as it seemed that Pierre was becoming somewhat inappropriate in his conversation.

Pierre then abruptly switched gears, and suddenly decided to give Micah relationship advice, telling him clichés such as "Don't go to bed angry," and "Always be honest with each other."

After some awkward silence, and after some visible reflection on Pierre's face, he said sternly, "There may be things that you discover that I have done...or that Cassandra's mother may have done that you may not agree with. But you must remember that at the end of the day, I am the father, and we are always going to be the parents."

Micah remained silent. He was unsure what to make of this statement. Was he referring to the sexual abuse? Was he trying to assert that parents, or he himself, can do no wrong?

His arrogance made Micah wonder if he had other victims out there; he wondered if he sexually abused my sister, Sorelle, as a baby. The cause of his split from her mother was unknown. As Micah sat in silence, with thoughts of potential hidden messages floating around in his head, father started discussing his issues.

He rambled on about he was getting older and was unable to do the things he used to do. He talked about how the glaucoma has been affecting his eyesight and about his aching back.

Micah zoned out. He was wrapped up in Pierre's previous statement. What on earth did he mean by what he had said?

While Micah was having a man-to-man with my father, I was having a woman-to-woman with Brianna. She wanted to talk about my plans, and I could tell by her tone of voice and her subtle suggestions that staying at her house for an entire month would be a strain on her household.

After so many hints, she finally confirmed that with the summer heat and so many people residing in her home currently, with only one bathroom, it would not be possible for her to house me for the entire grace-period. She said that she could, however, host me for short periods of time, perhaps weekends, if I could alternate between homes. I knew she was right; I'd be infringing too much on her family, and had to look into other options.

When Micah left for the plane back home, the countdown was really on. I had a lot of things to get together. Although I had decided to give both Mom and myself time to work things out after I disclosed the sexual abuse face-to-face, it was uncertain that we'd even get the chance. I needed to be able to see Teti, to spend more time with my brother, and allow my mother time to get over her shock and move into whatever action she chose. I needed to be available to help her with whatever change she chose to make.

I wanted to at least have the option of being available. If she wanted to make moves, I was ready to make it happen. I could help her shop for a small 2-bedroom apartment, which she could share with Troy. I could help her pack her belongings, and look into a good lawyer. I would make calls to the family, letting them know that she needed support. I would find a therapist in the area for her, so that she could process her shock and heartbreak. I would spend time with her, answering any unanswered questions she might have. I wanted all of us to support one another—me, Troy and Mom, together.

I had to find an alternative place to stay, and I needed to find it quick. Due to the poor economy, unfortunately, all of my friends were still living at home with their parents and siblings, which limited my options significantly.

JUNE 26TH 2011 (12 DAYS TIL D-DAY)

I decided to ask my good friend from high school, Keket. Since my graduation from graduate school, our communication became more frequent and our friendship grew stronger. She also lived near my house, which meant that if I stayed with her, I would have easier access to my brother. I did not disclose my reason for wanting to stay at her home, only that I needed to spend time there due to family conflict. Unfortunately, the timing was problematic for Keket.

Keket was right in the middle of studying for her bar exam, which made it a very anxious and intense time for her; she could afford zero distractions. Furthermore, her mother, who was mildly aware of the conflict I had with my parents, did not want to be involved or get in the middle of things, and instead insisted that it would be best that I work out whatever differences I had with my mother. As far as she knew, it was something that with some effort could be easily resolved. It quickly became evident that if I were to stay at anyone's home, I would have some sort of explaining to do, and I wasn't ready to do that.

My plans had to change. Having a grace period was no longer an option. That meant that instead of almost two months, I only had a few weeks to say goodbye to my friends and my brother. It broke my heart.

I had gotten very used to spending my mornings with Troy. Every morning, we would get each other out of bed, go out to the track and run together. He was my coach and would push me to run hard like I used to when I ran track in high school. Afterwards, we'd relax by preparing and eating a healthy breakfast together, followed by lounging around since the parents were at work. I hadn't prepared for my plan to fall through and for my time to be cut short with him. I wasn't ready to say goodbye.

I contemplated postponing the disclosure, but it was not a viable option. The tension in the house had risen to the point that even Troy could barely wait for the issues to be put out in the open, so we would no longer have to continue "playing nice." No one had said anything to one another, yet the overabundance of suppressed emotions was suffocating. It hung in the air like humidity, and you could feel its angry stickiness on your skin. You could taste the bitterness on your tongue. You could smell the rotting stench. It had permeated through the entire house. Mother had said nothing. Pierre acted as if everything was normal, but would do passive-aggressive things like putting the trashcan behind Troy's car, or put his run-down work shoes on Troy's sneakers, little things that he knew would annoy Troy. He puffed out his chest just a little more than usual. Troy buried himself with work and social activities, and was otherwise locked in his room. I observed my nerves tingling, bracing myself for an explosion.

My hands were tied, and I had to make the decision. Postponing the date of disclosure would not change the fact that there would be no grace period—it was simply delaying the inevitable. July 8th, 2011 would be the day I would disclose my sexual abuse to my mother, and it would also be the day that I would move out of the house and down to Georgia with Micah. I would offer her my support over the phone, and if need be, I would fly back as many times as was needed to speak to her and support her in person.

As for Troy, I would introduce myself to Ronny's family—with whom he would be staying—to ensure that it was a good environment and to provide them with my information so that they may directly contact me in any case of emergency.

I picked up my phone and sent a mass text message to all of my friends: "Meet me at The Cherry Pit next Friday at 9. It will be our last get-together before I move to Georgia!!"

JUNE 27ᵀᴴ 2011 (D-DAY MINUS 11)

Troy and I had a few errands that we had to take care of prior to D-day. First we headed to the post office. We made sure to have our mail forwarded to our new addresses immediately so that the post office would have a week to get into the groove of sending our mail to a new location.

We then headed to Rutgers to confirm whether Pierre had filled out a FAFSA for Troy's classes for the next semester, which he had not. So we added to the To-Do list that I would assist him in filing for federal aid for school, and for a loan if necessary.

Finally, we headed to our cell phone provider's store to find out how to block phone numbers. Father was not a person that we wanted to see or hear from, particularly after D-day. As a matter of fact, from that point on, he wasn't our father; he was simply a man named Pierre Baptiste. Severing connections and cutting ties was crucial to us moving forward. After handling our errands, we treated ourselves to lunch at a local food spot and discussed our anticipations for D-day.

I felt some guilt about the effect that my situation would have on Troy's relationship with Mom. I had of course expected for there to be anger and animosity towards Pierre, but I had no idea what to expect with how Troy would see Mom. I myself was struggling with my feelings towards her. Troy was not one to openly express his emotions, as a typical nineteen-year-old male. He was extremely guarded, particularly for what are considered "softer" emotions, such as hurt, sadness, worry, etc.

Troy was very proud of his astrological sign, which is Leo, representing strength, pride, and potentially stoicism. The combination of Troy's need to represent all that is "Leo" and all that is "man" made it at times difficult to get to the root of what he was truly feeling. I knew him well enough to know that what he would present on the outside was not equivalent to the emotions buried inside, so I had to tactfully ask him questions. Conversation was best facilitated over food.

"How do you feel about Mom and Dad and this whole situation?" I asked as I dove into my hot wings.

"Well, obviously, I've closed the book on Pierre. He raped you."

I cringed. I never attributed the word "rape" with what happened to me. Maybe it sounded too harsh. There was something about that word that made me sick to my stomach, more so than "sexual abuse."

I looked at Troy, and in a pleading voice, I asked, "Troy, why do you have to use that word?"

He seemed annoyed at my request. "Cassandra, you need to say things as they are. That's what happened. You can't just sugar coat things. You need to be blunt and honest."

I thought about how he was technically correct, since what Pierre did is legally called "statutory rape," but the word itself—*rape*—sounded filthy. Just saying it in my mind left me with a profound sense of contamination. I thought of ripped clothes, dark alleyways, physical abuse and screams.

That wasn't me. I wasn't a rape victim. Or was I? In a sense, the term "child sexual abuse" was a euphemistic phrase... not that it was pretty in any way, but in my mind, it was far easier on the ears than the harshness of "rape."

But, I thought to myself, *Troy is right*. It might not have looked like the typical *Law & Order* rape in an alleyway, but it was certainly rape. It was rape in the way he took advantage of his power as my father and as an adult to abuse me. It was rape in the way that he manipulated my young mind, telling me stories and lies so that I would go along. It was rape in the way he exposed me to pornographic images at such a young age. And most of all, what he did to my body was undeniably rape.

I snapped out of my thoughts and focused on asking Troy questions.

"What do you think about Mom?"

"I dunno," he shrugged as he put a French fry in his mouth, "We'll see how she reacts when you tell her, although I don't have much faith in her."

We continued eating in silence. I patiently waited for more; I knew better than to push.

Finally he said, "You know, I don't have any trust in people."

"What do you mean?" I asked.

"I feel like I've been lied to my whole life. They still haven't told me about you being adopted."

Wow, I thought to myself. It had never dawned on me that it was still an issue for him. I had assumed that by telling him myself, the truth was out, and he was in the know. Yet, he was still waiting on our parents to tell him, even though it had become clear to him that they had no intention of doing so.

He continued, "Sometimes, I wonder: what if I was born with some strange illness or disease? Would they just keep it from me?"

Troy wasn't kidding when he said he doesn't trust. I wanted to say, "I know how you feel," but I honestly didn't—my experiences were different than his. Yet, my heart went out to him. I had already made sense of my lack of trust due to my sexual abuse, but I had failed to consider what Troy's life was like. It's sad to imagine him wondering what lie he would uncover next.

"Well, you know you'll always have me to tell you the truth no matter what," I said, hoping that it could comfort him, but inside I knew that the feeling of betrayal in his heart would never disappear.

I thought about how I discovered that my mother had diabetes last year. She had called me into her room to help her program her glucose-testing device. I assumed that it was for work, since she was a nurse. But when I looked at the boxes containing the test strips, I saw her name under the prescription.

"Mom, why do you have to test your blood?"

She casually replied, "Because I have diabetes."

I felt absolutely hurt that she did not come to me or my brother to divulge such important medical information. I was also disappointed that the communication barrier between us was readily apparent.

The thought passed as our waitress asked if we were doing okay. I nodded, and she hurried off to another table. I looked up at Troy.

"You know, I have to practice what I'm going to say to Mom on D-day," I said. "I haven't prepared at all—it seems so surreal that it's actually happening."

"Yeah, you should," he replied. "You can practice with me."

"Good idea," I said. "What are *you* going to say to her?" I followed up.

"Nothing," he nonchalantly replied.

I brushed it off as Troy not wanting to plan out what to say. He often said, "I'll deal it when I get to it" in reference to questions about future planning.

To clarify, I asked, "What do you mean 'nothing,' Troy?"

"*Nothing*," he replied.

I gave him a stare, indicating that he needed to elaborate.

"She doesn't deserve the luxury of me having a conversation with her..."

"Troy," I said in a serious tone, "Is this all because of what happened to me? You can't just write her off like that." I couldn't sit with the feeling that I was responsible for the deterioration of his relationship with Mom.

"No," he frowned and shook his head. "The issues were already there, with both Mom and Dad...Your situation was just icing on the cake."

I felt somewhat assuaged, but I still wanted to know what else Troy experienced that made him feel so strongly.

He continued, "Do you remember the time I made that Clara Barton project?"

I nodded. I vaguely remembered; it was when he was much younger, maybe elementary school.

"I worked so hard on that project, especially because I thought she would be so proud since it was about a nurse... And then I practiced my presentation for her, and she just laughed at me. Remember, I went into your room and cried on your shoulder afterwards, and all she did was stay in her room, yelling, 'Why is he crying.' She didn't care that she hurt my feelings... I worked *so* hard on that project."

Wow. I hadn't even known that that specific incident was so monumental to him. I remember oftentimes comforting him when he was younger simply because Mom wasn't around or was unavailable, and it was typically prompted by Pierre's harshness in discipline. I could feel the disappointment and hurt that Troy felt as a child, and it amazed me that those feelings remained strong despite years of elapsed time.

"Fuck her," he expressed vehemently, slamming his fist hard on the table, causing the drinks to shake. "She never protected us. Anytime there was a conflict between us and Pierre, she would always take his side, just like she did when Pierre got in my face about the mail and hit me. She's never cared about how I feel." He shook his head disappointedly.

I could not refute his point. I had not expressed it, but I felt the same way. It was eye-opening for me to see that although Troy and I had completely different experiences with our parents, we had come to the same conclusions about them. I could only frown and shrug.

18

⌒⌒⌒⌒

JUNE 28TH 2012 (D-DAY MINUS 10)

I was overwhelmed with the ceaseless planning and stress-
ors related to the disclosure. My world was consumed with
thoughts and fears related to the disclosure. My escape was
watching movies. I had a shared Netflix account with Micah,
which provided hundreds of movies at my fingertips. I had
watched full seasons of TV shows and all of the movies that
seemed intriguing.

That day, I decided to watch an old horror movie for kicks.
Old horror movies were amusing; they typically weren't scary
at all due to lack of technology for special effects. I randomly
selected an eighties cult classic, and as I started to watch, there
was something familiar about it. I quickly brushed it off, as there
were many horror films that took place in a cabin in the woods.

I continued to watch, until one particular scene, in which a
person gets violently stabbed, placed me where I had previously watched this film. It was in my father's bedroom during one
of those late nights. As I watched it years later, I could only recognize two of the scenes, but I was aghast at the inappropriate

amount of gore and horror in the film that would surely terrify any ten-year-old.

I couldn't help but wonder if exploiting my fear was a tactic to keep me awake and terrorized. I knew that I would never understand his motive and his tactics, but I realized that I may also never fully know what happened to me, and I may spend the rest of my life experiencing flashbacks, triggered by various things, whether it's a movie, a color, a scent, anything.

JUNE 29TH 2011 (D-DAY MINUS 9)

One of the most important things I needed to do was make sure that I had all of my documents for the move. I needed both me and my brother's birth certificates, social security cards, passports, and any other necessary documents.

Everyone's paperwork, however, was in my father's possession. I had seen him, on numerous occasions, remove stacks of manila folders from one of his dresser drawers whenever I requested my own documents in the past. It wouldn't be hard to find which drawer contained what I was looking for.

I prepared for this task by having a copy of their room key made without their knowledge. When it was time to make my move, Troy served as a lookout. Even though the parents were off at work, it wasn't uncommon for Pierre to show up randomly because he forgot something or simply to use the bathroom.

Once I entered the room, I went straight to the drawer filled with documents. It was tedious work. I had to sift through what seemed like mountains of manila folders. I had to ensure that nothing was left misplaced, and my fingers throbbed where they served as placeholders for stacks of paper that I had already sorted through.

Finally, I came across Troy's birth certificate. Check. Then my immunization record. Check; I would definitely need that. After some time, I found both of our passports and Troy's social security card. Check, check, and check. Troy was clear; all of his documents had been found.

I could not find my birth certificate. I hoped it would stick out as I quickly thumbed through stacks and stacks of papers. I saw mortgage papers, my adoption paperwork, and tax information—but then something caught my eye. I found my biological father's death certificate.

His death was something that I was always curious about. I assumed that he was close to my mother's age, and since he passed away while I was so young, I worried if he had any physical ailments that could have been passed on to me. The way that my mother informed me, she simply said, "He was sick and died."

As was customary in our house, conversation regarding my biological father was not condoned. My mother had referred to him only twice in my life: when she told me that the man she was married to was not my father, and when she informed me that the man she was married to would be adopting me due to my biological father's death.

I quickly scanned the death certificate for his cause of death as my heart rate quickened and beat harder in my chest. This was my chance to get *real* information.

His name was Yves Pierre. He passed away at the young age of 49 years old. The certificate stated that the immediate cause of death was "pending." The manner of death was "pending further study." That meant that they were unsure if it was natural, accidental, a homicide, or a suicide. An autopsy was performed; there had to be some sort of clue as to how he died.

I became more focused as I tried to draw conclusions based on the limited information I could glean from one sheet of paper. His profession was identified as "auto mechanic." Perhaps he had an accident at work? There was no way of knowing. I brought my eyes back to the top of the page and noticed that the "Place of Death" indicated that my biological father passed away in Brooklyn, New York. I paused. *Brooklyn, New York?* That didn't make any sense.

I clearly remembered in the first conversation I had with my mother that she said, "He's living in Florida with his family." I started to feel a not-so-good feeling in the pit of my stomach—a feeling that I had been lied to. I searched for more information. The certificate stated that he had resided in New Castle, New York. Clearly, he was not a Floridian. The uneasiness in my stomach turned to anger.

Wow, I thought, *What was the purpose in Mom lying to me about where he lived? That is just unnecessary.*

I made sure to read every single line on that certificate, not once but twice, just to ensure that I didn't miss any information. Among the last lines of the death certificate, I read, "Name of Cemetery or Crematory: Rosehill Cemetery" followed by "Location: Linden, NJ."

My eyes froze where they were. Linden, New Jersey was no more than twenty minutes away from my house. My biological father was buried practically around the corner, and my mother had led me to believe that he lived and died in Florida! I felt the anger in my belly turn to rage. That was my last straw with Mother.

I called Troy into the room and showed him the certificate. I had become overwhelmed with the same feeling that Troy had expressed to me a few days earlier, the feeling that things had been kept from me—that I had been lied to my whole life. I felt that I had a right to know that information. I should have been told the absolute truth, even if not at a young age, at least when I had gotten older.

Parents try to protect their kids while they're young and fill their minds with nice stories and fairytales, but when the children grow up, they must learn that Santa Claus is not real and that the Easter Bunny did not exist. I didn't feel that I was being protected. I was being conned, deceived, lied to and manipulated by both of my parents, and I was furious.

My search for documents ended for the day, and I went to my room to process this newfound information. What I had found that day raised a lot of questions, and to this day I still do not have most of the answers.

JUNE 30TH, 2011 (D-DAY MINUS 8)

I came to the conclusion that although I never got to know my father, it would only be fair for me to pay my respects to him at his grave site prior to moving several states away. It felt wrong to leave without saying goodbye. Troy volunteered to accompany me to his burial site.

I went to the store and purchased some roses. I searched for the cemetery address, punched it into my GPS and headed to the location. I thought to myself how thankful I was to have a little brother. I realized that in times like this, when I needed support, he was there in the role of a big brother. It's not something that he would readily admit, but he truly was a loving and caring individual, one who I could depend on.

Once we reached the gravesite, after fifteen minutes of searching, we found the location that corresponded to the letters and numbers on his death certificate. It was an unmarked site, causing me to feel empty and disappointed. I had a small hope to perhaps learn something from his tombstone. But there was nothing, a dead end for me. It was a square patch of dirt. I felt bad because I felt that everyone, no matter who they are, should have something, anything, besides a plot of dry dirt for people to remember them by.

The experience made me speculate even further about my biological father's character. Did his family feel that he didn't deserve a tombstone? Was he that kind of man? Maybe they could not afford the expense of a tombstone.

I wondered about his family, whom he had left behind, whether I had other brothers and sisters, and what kind of people they were. Logically, I couldn't have attained such information just from visiting his gravesite, but there was something inside me that hoped to somehow get closer to, or understand, the man I came from. I said a few words and laid down a few roses for the father I never got to know.

That night I had a nightmare. I dreamt that I was in Georgia and had started working at a new job in a big office building. While at work, Pierre appeared in the doorway to my cubicle. I froze, terrified, unsure how he found me. I had taken the precautions to cover my tracks so well, but alas, there he was, standing over me. His eyes were wolfish—uncaring, brutal— and I was his prey. He said he had been watching me for days. He found out where I lived and followed me to my job. Mother had left him, and he had nothing. He wanted to punish me for speaking out against him. He wanted to take everything away from me, as he blamed me for doing so to him. Then he lunged at me, eyes wild, arms outstretched. I quickly grabbed a metal fork from my desk and plunged it into his neck. As the fork made impact, I woke up with a stiff jolt.

I lay there on my back, in the dark, panicked, thinking, *What if this really happens?*

What if Mom leaves him, and he becomes angry and vengeful, with his sole purpose to torture me for outing him? My life would become a living horror movie. I tried to push the thoughts out of my mind and go back to sleep, but the dream had left me completely rattled.

JULY 2ND, 2011 (D-DAY MINUS 6)

I still needed my birth certificate, and, again with Troy as the lookout, I resumed my search. In the process, I stumbled across more surprising information. I found a marriage certificate dated December 1985 and divorce papers in October 1987 between my mother and biological father.

Who was this woman called my mother? It was not that I had ever expected for her to tell me that she had once been married and divorced, but it was yet another fact that was cached away.

I had always assumed that I was born out of wedlock and that my biological father left my mom and ignored his responsibility to me. Also, divorce is not something that is common among Haitian women, which made it even more shocking and unexpected. Troy looked at it as a possible sign that she is a person who is open to divorce, so maybe she would be more likely to leave Pierre after my disclosure, but I was skeptical.

I was born in April 1986, only leading me to the seemingly obvious conclusion that my mother had a shotgun wedding due to an unplanned pregnancy with me. I imagined that my religious grandmother would have zero tolerance for a grandchild born out of wedlock. Who knows if they were even in love? Perhaps it wasn't an accident and wedding plans were already in their future.

Maybe neither of them foresaw the divorce that would occur a year and a half after I was born. My mom did not ask for any child support in the divorce paperwork. It stated, "The defendant shall have reasonable rights of visitation." There were never any visits that I could recall, but I was told that my biological father refused to sign adoption papers while he was alive, which is why the adoption happened after he passed away. I wondered why he never signed those papers. Did he want a relationship with me as a daughter? Was it a macho pride thing, and he didn't want another man's name attached to his child? Or did he know Pierre, and know what an evil man he was? After much speculation, I then pondered how Mother would feel about me asking her to leave her current husband, because he sexually abused me.

In her world, I would be seen as the recurring problem in her life. I thought about it: she was forced into a marriage because of an unexpected pregnancy with me, and now she would feel forced to end her marriage of over 20 years to her second husband, because of me. She could easily decide that she's made enough sacrifices and decide to let me go. It was a sad thought, but it was a very real possibility.

JULY 3rd 2011 (D-DAY MINUS 5)

It was the 4th of July weekend, and Ronny's family was having a barbeque. This was an opportunity for me to meet Troy's surrogate family. Of course, I was nervous seeing them because one week prior, they'd had a sit-down conversation with Troy and had speculated that the reason for Troy's sudden move was because I had been sexually abused. Troy's friend, Ronny, had only told his parents that Troy could no longer stay in his home because his father had done something unspeakable. After further conversation with Troy, they verified that their hypothesis was accurate and opened their home and hearts to him.

I walked into their home with Troy, and everyone greeted him with enthusiasm. They were excited to see him, and he fit right in as if he belonged there. The mother greeted me very warmly and offered me food and drink. Troy easily slipped into conversation with the guys about sports and typical guy stuff. I sat and sipped some wine while surveying the area.

The bookshelf was filled with books. This meant that they were avid readers, which was a good sign. The house was clean and organized, with an aura of comfort. On the fridge, there were newspaper clippings warning teens not to text and drive.

The parents appeared to be friendly and down to earth. The mother in particular had a nurturing personality about her, making sure that everyone was having a good time, engaging in conversation, offering everyone food and drink. I felt a good vibe there, and felt that Troy was going to be okay.

Before we left, I took the mom aside to thank her greatly for taking Troy into her home.

She responded, "I couldn't turn him away. He's like a son to me."

I held back tears.

She added, "Please, do not hesitate to call me if you need anything."

I gave her a warm hug and thanked her again for her hospitality. I had to thank God for blessing both Troy and I with such great people. They were angels, and it was a small miracle that Troy had them in his life.

JULY 4TH 2011 (D-DAY MINUS 4)

Mother and Pierre had decided to have a small barbeque of their own. At one point, I made mixed drinks for my uncle and myself.

Upon seeing this, Pierre demanded, "What did I do to you for you to treat me like this? I am sitting here hot and sweaty, but you don't offer your own father something to drink."

All that was missing was the world's smallest violin.

Mom immediately fell for the bait and jumped in, "Why didn't you get your father something? Why are you so mean to him?"

I let out a sigh and didn't respond.

JULY 7TH 2011 (D-DAY MINUS 1)

My trunk was packed full of my belongings. It was so full that the back end of my car had dropped inches lower than the front end. Over the past few months, I had packed and shipped numerous boxes to Micah. The rest of my belongings, I had packed in bins and stacked in the basement of the house.

I feared that my parents would notice that many of my things were packed and put away in a special corner, but they never mentioned a word to me. Troy did inform me that Mother randomly asked him a while back if I had plans to move out, but he had suggested that she speak to me directly. She never came to me. Either Mother was oblivious or she simply didn't care. Nobody pointed out that my keyboard had vanished, or that my room started to look rather sparse. My closet was completely empty, except for a few lonely hangers that dangled from the rod.

Troy and I sat outside by the pool discussing D-Day, which was less than 24-hours away. Still, I felt nothing: no fear, no anxiety—nothing. We decided to role-play what it would be like for me to tell Mother. Troy volunteered to play her.

"Mom, I need to talk to you," I started.

"What do you want? I'm busy and tired from work," Troy replied, in an annoyed high-pitched voice. He had gotten into character, leaning back, eyes straight ahead as if he were watching TV, air-remote in hand.

"But this is important..." I continued.

"Okay. Hurry. I have my show to watch. Brenda is coming back from the dead on *General Hospital*."

I couldn't help but laugh. His impersonation of her was quite accurate. "Okay, let's fast-forward to the meat of the convo. Umm...how do I say it?"

"Honestly, I don't know. Go easy but get to the point," He replied.

"Your husband is a pedophile," I said with a shrug.

"Uhh...I don't think you should start like that. That's a bit harsh," he said.

"Okay...so should I start like, 'When I was five...'"

He shrugged, seemingly not content with that route either.

"What if she says something like, 'You're a liar! I don't believe you!'" I asked.

Troy immediately switched roles, playing me and replying, "Why would I make up this lie now?"

"Because you're a good-for-nothing liar," I said aggressively, getting into her character.

"Oooh!" Troy exclaimed, unprepared for a response. "That would be the end of that conversation. I would be so pissed I'd want to strangle her."

"Yeah—well, that wasn't the best preparation, huh?" I joked.

But in all seriousness, there seemed to be no real way to prepare for this discussion. Perhaps she would believe me. Perhaps she'd yell at me. Perhaps she'd slap me. There was no way of knowing.

JULY 8ᵀᴴ 2011 (D-DAY)

I woke up and thought to myself, *today is the day*. I didn't particularly feel any kind of way. It was 8:45. I looked out the window and saw Pierre walk towards his car carrying his briefcase, as if it were an ordinary Friday.

"Goodbye, Asshole!" I said as I watched him drive away.

Brianna, who had slept over the night before, looked at me in disproval of my remark. She probably thought I wasn't taking the significance of today seriously. I shrugged. I was more worried about cramming the rest of my belongings into my car. My closet was already emptied, but I had to focus on breaking down my little bookcase and finding a way to fit it into my car. I must've added a couple hundred pounds to it already.

I prayed that it would be able to handle the 800-mile drive to Georgia. Troy got up and came into my room saying "Ready?" as if it was a typical morning where we would go for a run together. Clearly, this morning was different.

He and I made multiple trips to and from the house, carrying armfuls of our personal items to our vehicles, with Brianna's help. It had become less like loading and more like a Tetris puzzle: finding little nooks and crannies to wiggle objects in, rotating objects at certain angles to make more space. It soon became evident that I wouldn't be able to see out of my rearview mirror.

All of us had worked up a hunger from the heavy lifting and loading of cars. Ronny came over, and we all decided to go to IHOP for some breakfast. I got into my over-stuffed car with Brianna and Troy rode with Ronny.

As I pulled out of the driveway, I put in one of the CD's that Troy had made for me for the long trip to Georgia. As soon as the first track started playing, it struck my soul with such intense sorrow that I was completely unprepared for.

Troy tended to listen to a rotation of six to ten songs of what I would personally categorize as "emo" music: very "I am alone in this world," "my soul hurts," and "the world is a dark place." But it wasn't the message in the songs that struck me with such emotional vengeance. It was that this was *Troy's* music.

I was used to only hearing it in his presence, and listening to his music without him—even for the short fifteen-minute drive to IHOP—brought heavy nostalgia into my soul. I felt hot tears burning in the back of my eyeballs. I blinked and looked up to try to keep them at bay.

Brianna adjusted her seat next to me, and my heart dropped deep into my belly as my attention was drawn to her. A huge lump invaded in my throat. I realized that I was also leaving a friend whom I had allowed to be closer to me than any other friend before her; she had become my adopted sister.

"Shit," I thought to myself, "Why does this hurt so much?" The intense emotion caught me like a deer in headlights. I had been perfectly fine only a few minutes prior.

I turned off the music, but by then it was too late. The lump in my throat made it difficult for me to even swallow. I had just pulled into the IHOP parking lot when the tears spilled like a waterfall over the rims of my eyelids. I put the car into park and doubled-over.

The pain was so great that I was gasping for air. It was like my body was at war with itself. It felt like my soul wanted to expel its pain from my body, causing me to cry out heavily in anguish, propelling my body forward. I had to gasp for air to fill my empty lungs. It hurt physically, emotionally, and spiritually.

The pain that hadn't seemed to be present throughout weeks of preparation, up until that morning, had finally manifested itself. Brianna and Troy comforted me, but there didn't seem to be any going back. Troy wiped the flowing tears from my bloodshot eyes with his shirt. "I don't want to leave you!" I screeched, in between violent sobs, my words muffled in his chest.

"I'm going to be okay, Cassy...I'm going to be okay," he reassured me, "This is something you have to do. And we had to part ways sometime."

Eventually, I calmed down, but whoever said crying makes you feel better must've lied because I felt miserable. We all walked into the restaurant where I only ate a few bites of an omelet. My appetite had vanished, and although the tears had stopped flowing, I was an emotional wreck.

I returned to the house after saying goodbye to Brianna and dropping her off at the train station. Troy went to his new home, to set up his new room, to get settled in. The house felt particularly empty, eerily empty.

On the dining room table, there were two house keys and the car key to the car my brother had been borrowing to get around. Troy's room was empty, and his walls that were once covered with posters and pictures were now bare as if no one had ever resided in that room.

I sat in my room, alone, on my bed and in silence, looking outside, and waiting for my mother's car to pull into the driveway. The house was completely dark and silent, as if the world had frozen around me. I could feel my heart beating through my summer dress. I leaned on the windowsill and waited for two o'clock, checking every thirty seconds. Sometimes she would get home sooner; sometimes she would get home later.

I looked into the sky and saw the clouds start to change. It seemed that the weather was ominous. What had been a beautiful sunny day was quickly turning into a dark and rainy one. The clouds started moving faster as the wind picked up and the sun disappeared. I heard thunder rumbling in the distance.

I drearily muttered, "How dramatic."

It was like God was setting the stage. Shortly after the thundering began, my mother pulled into the driveway.

I watched as she used a magazine to shield her head from the fat raindrops that fell from the sky. I quickly ran from my room to the living room to greet my mother. As I sat on the couch in the living room, facing the large windows, I saw a flash of lightning. It was the slowest flash of lightning I had ever seen. I saw the jagged bolt of brilliant light reach down from the sky and pierce the air before disappearing. I heard the key turn in the door and held my breath as my mom pushed the door open.

"Hi, Mom," I said as she reached the top of the stairs.

"Hi," she replied, as she whirled around, apparently startled by my presence in the now darkened living room.

"How was work?" I asked, figuring I should be polite before dropping the bomb I had in store for her.

"Good...Are you going somewhere?" She had sensed that my behavior was different. Sitting stiffly in the living room while holding onto my keys was not how I typically greeted my mother.

"Yeah, I'm going out. I need to talk to you, Mom." I had decided to get right to the point.

Without question, she walked over to me, still holding the large bag that she carried to work in one hand and the wet magazine in the other. She sat on the couch adjacent to mine. I was caught off guard at her immediate willingness to sit and listen to me. I expected the usual excuse that she was tired, or that she had more important things to do, but not this time. I had her full attention.

My heart started to pound even harder, which I didn't think was possible. I looked down at the keys as in my hands and nervously slid one key at a time from one key ring to another.

"Me and Troy are leaving."

"Where are you going?"

She must've thought I was going to the store or something.

"Georgia," I replied, as if it was the name of a street around the corner. I continued, "As for Troy, you're going to have to talk to him."

And then came the big question:

"Why?" she asked, strangely in a very calm manner.

I hesitated and pursed my lips together, taking a deep breath before I could let the next sentence escape my lips. I looked up from my keys.

"Dad is a pedophile," I said quietly.

"A pedophile?"

Maybe that wasn't the best choice of words. Maybe she didn't understand what that meant.

I clarified, "A child sexual abuser."

"Sexual abuse?" she echoed in disbelief. "To who?"

"To me," I replied, in a voice that shockingly came out sounding like a little girl.

"Pierre?" She asked again, pointing to the empty hallway as if he were standing there.

"Yes," I replied, more confidently this time.

"When did this happen?" She had started speaking Creole.

It was her default language, particularly when she was especially emotional or didn't feel comfortable articulating what she had to say in English.

"At night when you would go to work."

She looked at me with an emotionless stare. I silently cursed the storm outside, as I searched for some sort of expression on her face in the dark room. My mother's eyes—though I could barely make them out—never left me; she sat frozen, still clutching onto her bag and her wet magazine. I looked down uncomfortably and continued fiddling with my keys, listening to the sound of the rain hitting the pavement outside.

Maybe I hadn't answered her question.

I continued, "It started since Philadelphia."

"But you were only ten then."

I looked up from my keys. Maybe she really wasn't grasping the concept of a child sexual abuser.

"He started when I was six," I said and felt my brows furrow.

"He touched your breasts?"

"Yes," I winced, fearing that she would ask me about explicit details, as Troy had.

"He had sex with you?"

"Yes."

After a brief silence, she asked again, "Pierre?"

Apparently it was hard to believe. But she seemed to be taking it well. I was no longer worried about her attacking me or going ballistic. It was evident that she was not processing the information; she was in shock. I hadn't prepared for that reaction.

"Who else have you told this?" she asked.

"Just Troy," I lied. I didn't feel it was necessary for her to know that she was further down on the list of people I had already told.

We sat in an uncomfortable silence again. It seemed endless, and I cleared my throat although I didn't need to. I guess it was up to me to break the silence again.

I asked, "So what are you going to do?"

Still, silence.

I had fully rearranged all of my keys to one key ring, and my membership cards to another ring. I figured that made sense, because it was annoying to have to fumble to find my Pathmark or Shoprite or Borders card when it was hidden in between my keys. I stared at what I had done, wondering if I should rearrange them again, and she finally spoke.

"Since you're older now and he can't hurt you anymore, why leave?"

I looked up at her, squinting my eyes, searching her face, and trying to read her expression to understand what she meant by her question. I couldn't read anything. Again, I cursed the darkness, as if the light would have revealed some subtle expression that was hidden on her face somewhere. Was she saying that she believed me? But if she did, why would she ask me such a ludicrous question?

I replied with a question of my own, "Do you expect me to continue to stay here after what he's done to me?"

Silence again. It was becoming annoyingly unbearable. What was I supposed to say? What was I supposed to do? Should I keep my distance, or should I console her? Did she even need any consolation?

I found myself filling the silence, rambling, "I didn't tell you earlier because I was young...and I was confused...and at one point I thought you knew...so I wasn't going to tell...but then I decided I would tell once I'm out of the house, safe and away from him..."

Still, silence.

Shoot, I thought to myself, *Maybe I shouldn't have said that I thought she knew. I didn't want to put forth a sense of blame.*

The silence was killing me. I needed her to give me *something*, anything.

So I asked again, "Sooo, what are you going to do?"

Again, nothing.

We sat in silence for what seemed like half an hour, although it was probably no more than ten minutes. Mom looked like a statue. She hadn't moved a muscle—not in her body and surely not in her face.

Finally after concluding that there was nothing more to say, and not knowing what else to do, I said, "Well, I guess I'll go now," hoping to snap her out of her zombie-like state.

She snapped out of her trance long enough to ask, "Where are you going now?"

"To a hotel."

I wasn't leaving for Georgia until the next morning. I hoped that maybe she would give me some sort of response, knowing that I was leaving, but still nothing. I took a deep breath and looked her in her eyes, which at the moment appeared so lifeless.

I said, "Just because I'm leaving doesn't mean that I'm not available. You have my number and Troy's number, which you can call anytime. You just need to tell me what you want to do and I can always fly right back up here." Oddly, I felt the need to console and support her, although I had initially hoped for the same from her, since I was the one who lived through the sexual abuse.

She made no indication that she wanted or needed my support. She offered only silence.

"Okay. Goodbye, Mom," I said, giving her one last lingering gaze, letting her know that I was really leaving, and that if she had anything to say, she should say it right then.

Everything after that seemed to happen in slow motion. I slowly leaned my body forward and lifted myself off the couch. I put my right foot in front of my left as the floor boards creaked beneath them. Mom stayed fixed on the area I had been sitting; not even her eyes followed me as I walked by.

As I passed her, I whispered, "Bye."

She didn't even so much as flinch.

I slowly walked down the stairs, waiting, praying for her head to peer over the banister at the last minute yelling, "Wait."

I opened the front door and reminded her to lock it since I no longer had a key. I slowly closed it and heard the latch click into the doorjamb. There was no going back. I let go of the doorknob and turned my back to the house.

I sat in my car, put my keys into the ignition, and just drove. I breathed out a sigh of relief. Well, I did it. I went through with it and came out alive. I called Troy and told him, "I did it," as if I was talking about a new haircut, nothing earth-shattering.

Immediately following the sense of relief was a sense of doubt. Was this all I had been preparing for? Did D-day just really happen for real, or had I been dreaming? It certainly felt like a dream. It was like I was out of touch with my body, like my hands weren't really touching the steering wheel, and like I wasn't really pressing the gas pedal. Things were just sort of happening.

I found myself grasping frantically for an understanding of what had just happened. I had no answer. She gave me no indication as to whether she believed me or not. I thought back to the image of my mother sitting on the couch like a statue. Had I abandoned her? Immediately I felt the same difficulty swallowing that I had felt that morning. Could I have comforted her; maybe given her a hug? I felt my throat swell, making it difficult to breathe. I couldn't believe I walked out when she could've possibly needed me the most.

I could barely see the road in front of me as tears flowed down my face. I felt like a complete bitch, feeling that I was inconsiderate for even telling my mother. I felt a sharp pain in my belly. What could I do? I couldn't un-say what I had already revealed to her.

"Shit," I yelled, slamming my hands against the steering wheel. I felt myself getting frustrated as I wiped my tears from my eyes. I had planned this for so long, yet I felt so incredibly lost.

I imagined my mother again, sitting in the living room. Was she still sitting there? Was she screaming? Was she crying? I had no idea. I didn't know anything anymore.

I pulled up to Troy's new home and sat in the car. I really hated crying. I didn't understand why it made your throat close up and your nostrils so stuffed you could barely breathe, and it gave you such a damn pounding headache. So you feel like shit before you start to cry, and then you cry, which causes you to feel even shittier.

I looked in my rearview mirror at my bloodshot eyes, contemplating my next move. I prayed that nobody was home. I wasn't in the mood to face anyone right now, but I needed to be with my brother. It was pouring outside, but I didn't care enough to get my umbrella.

⌬

Troy walked me into his new bedroom. He had already put his clothes away, hung up a few photos and set up his gaming systems. The room was small but comfortable. As soon as he shut the door, I became frantic.

"I left her. I left her all alone. I don't know what to do," I said as I sat down on his bed.

He asked me to slow down and to tell him what happened. He turned up the TV to provide us with some privacy from the thin walls.

After I explained the story, he suggested that we call her to see if she was okay. I pulled out my phone and nervously dialed her cell phone number.

"Hello," she answered. Her voice sounded so heavy and dry, as if she hadn't spoken in ages. I again wondered if she had been crying.

"Are you ok?" I asked. It sounded like such a dumb question, but I didn't know what to say, as I looked at Troy wide-eyed.

"Mmm-hmmm," she replied.

I felt a pang in my chest. It didn't sound genuine.

"Is there anything I can do?" I asked. Maybe now she was ready to talk and I would drive back to speak to her. Maybe I could even take Troy with me this time.

"No," she said.

In the background I heard Pierre's voice, "What's this? Did the kids move out or something?" He must've just walked in and seen all of the keys on the dining room table.

I panicked. "Okay. Bye," I said and quickly hung up the phone.

I looked at Troy and said, "He's there!"

She must've called him immediately after I left the house because it was less than half an hour later.

I followed up with a text message saying, "I am here for you. You can call me or Troy," giving her time and space to have the conversation with her husband.

Troy said, "Damn we messed up!"

I asked, "How so?"

He replied, "We should've put hidden cameras in that house."

PART II

19

When we watch movies, particularly thrillers, we love to put ourselves in the main character's shoes and imagine what we'd do differently. We love thinking that we're far more intelligent than the main character on the screen. We become experts at giving advice: "No! Don't go in there!" Or we boast about our superior intelligence: "What an idiot! I would have never done that!" We brainstorm with our fellow movie-watchers about what we would do differently to survive, especially in the apocalyptic-*Armageddon*-esque movies.

Luckily, when we are watching a TV show, a movie, or the news, we have the luxury of being presented with the individual's choices and the outcomes of those choices. We don't have that luxury in real life. I also believe that when we are presented with these "what if" scenarios, we like to place ourselves in an ideal world where we are fearless, courageous, invincible, and politically correct, especially when there is an audience waiting for an answer.

But let's say one of those "what if" scenarios that you only see on Lifetime movies, or on the news, becomes *your* real-life scenario. What if that storyline, that scene that you swear would never happen to you, becomes *your* story?

"I swear if someone did something like that to one of my kids...Oh I would make him pay; he would have to pay!" This was a statement said with confidence, and filled with strong anger. They were the words of my mother, in response to an Oprah show about child molesters.

The call I'd expected from my mother that evening never came. I waited and waited, felt my soul laden with guilt and gave into incessant tears, which I had given up on trying to control.

Two questions stuck in my mind: "Who else have you told this?" and "He can't hurt you anymore, so why leave?" Her concern over who I had told could be for one of two reasons. Either she was hurt for possibly being the last one to know, or she was more interested in assessing how much damage control she had to do. As for the second question, did that mean that she believed me, or was it hypothetical? Worse, did it mean that she had known all along, but it didn't matter?

I finally mustered up the courage to call her cell phone, again. I got no answer, nor did I get a call back. What if she went crazy and killed him? I paced around the hotel room I was in, wondering what I should do next. I wrote countless pages in my journal and cried endless tears. I was restless and unsure of what to do with myself until Micah's flight arrived, so I drove to Brooklyn to give a second farewell to Brianna.

We were able to joke and laugh, not focusing on the graveness of D-Day, and I suddenly felt the nostalgia of our college days. I remembered playing all types of games in our dorm room, going to parties, and going on adventures. After many hugs and a final goodbye, I left to pick up Micah at JFK Airport.

When I got there, his flight had already landed. I pulled up to the terminal and saw him standing by the curb. I was filled with joy, just seeing his smile, thinking of our future together. Yet there was also a finality about his presence. He represented the end of D-Day, but what did that even mean? It was unresolved, and I had many questions unanswered. I told him everything that had occurred. I quickly realized that I hadn't eaten much at all throughout the day. I felt nauseous, yet my stomach was growling. When we finally got back to my hotel, we ate snacks, watched TV, and fell asleep, recharging for the long drive the next day.

The next afternoon while in transit to Georgia, my mom texted me, "How are you are u there yet?"

I responded, "I should be there in 7 hrs. I'm more concerned about how you're doing. Just because I'm moving doesn't mean I'm unavailable to talk or visit if you need my support."

No answer. No call.

I figured I should give her some time to process her emotions. Three days later, I was completely unpacked but far from "settled" when she texted, "How are u?"

I replied, "Good. How are you?"

"Good thank u," she replied.

I wanted to TALK. I didn't want to have this spontaneous and polite chitchat like two strangers in passing. I became impatient and was angry with her for not calling me, for not acknowledging the conversation we had, for not being genuine in her "how are you" texts, which seemed more out of obligation than out of true affection. I understood that she may be in shock and that she might still be processing the information, but I wanted her to talk to me like I was her daughter and not a stranger.

I texted her back, "When do you want to talk on the phone?"

"Anytime," was her reply.

She didn't seem too anxious to call, so I responded, "Please call me when you're up to it." I wanted to talk to her when she was ready.

I didn't hear from her until ten days later. Actually, I hadn't heard from her at all; instead, I received a text saying, "Good Afternoon did u get my card?"

I checked my mailbox and opened up a card from Tender Thoughts that read:

> *When it seems like everything in your world is changing,*
> *You can always find comfort in the simple things,*
> *That have always been and will always be,*
> *Like the love and support of people who care.*
> *I'll always be here for you.*

Love, Mom.

What was I supposed to make of that card? She had not reached out to me for over a week, yet she sent me a card telling me that she loved me. I was confused and frustrated. Was this card a sign that she believed me? But if she did believe me, why wasn't she more proactive in speaking to me? I never would have guessed that D-day would be drawn out into D-weeks.

Every day I searched for answers—answers that would give me some insight into what was going on in my mother's head. How long did it take a person to process news like this? Were there statistics I should look up? Did she have an undercover plan to get her finances together for a couple of months before she decides to leave him? Did she plan to continue a relationship with him while still having a relationship with me? Maybe she just didn't believe me at all, but she was just being polite.

Regardless, I needed to have a conversation with her, a *real* conversation.

I responded with a text, "Thanks for the card. I will be calling soon." Clearly if I wanted answers, I would have to take the initiative.

The next day, when all was quiet, I finally decided to dial her number.

The phone rang, and she answered, "Hello?"

She sounded groggy.

"Hi, Mom," I said, "Were you sleeping?"

"No," she replied.

"Can you talk?" I asked. I needed her to be awake, alert, and focused.

"Yes, I can talk. How are you?" she said in a pleasant voice. Again with the formalities.

I replied, "I'm fine. I want to know how *you* are doing."

"I'm fine," she immediately replied.

"Do you need anything?" I asked, wondering if she would open up to me about how she was feeling, if she needed support of some sort.

"I'm fine. Do *you* need anything?"

I looked at the phone in my hand. Was there an echo? I felt the vein in my temple throb. It was like this was a game to her: who can be the most polite? I had hoped for a more genuine response. Perhaps, "Yes, this is really hard for me," or "I need you to help me find an apartment," or even, "I'm having difficulty understanding what you told me and I have some questions." I became quickly irritated at this polite game she was playing.

"Soo...what's going on?" It was time to be blunt and address the issue.

"Nothing," she replied, as if I had asked her casually what she had planned for her weekend.

I rolled my eyes and let out an exasperated breath. "Did-you-speak-to-him?" I said as I put emphasis on every syllable.

"MMMmmmmMM."

"Huh?" What kind of answer was that? She sounded like she had a stomachache.

Again, "Did you talk to him?" I made sure to articulate my words.

"Yes, but I don't want to talk about it over the phone."

I furrowed my brows. I guess it's fair to want to have this kind of conversation in person, but I shoved down my guilt for leaving and focused on what I was faced with: my mother on the phone, too uncomfortable to talk about what happened, with no desire to discuss it further.

"Okay...I understand," I said, "but this is something that we need to talk about, and since I don't have the money, I don't know when I will be back to talk about it in person." This was her cue to volunteer to visit me in Georgia, or even offer to split the cost for the plane ticket.

"Well...you'll figure it out," she casually replied.

You'll figure it out?! *You'll figure it out!?* I was enraged. Apparently, she seemed to feel that it was my problem, and not hers. She didn't seem interested at all in taking the initiative.

Before I could let my anger consume me, I said, "I have to go. I'm making lunch. Good bye."

"Good bye," she replied, calmly.

I paced around my new home for about ten minutes, and then I called back. I needed to know what her plan was. I refused to give up on her. I wanted to resolve this.

"Hello," she responded, "What did you have for lunch?"

"That doesn't matter," I said abruptly, "What if it takes me months to fly back to Jersey? You want to wait that long to discuss this?"

"Well...we'll see. We can look at the ticket prices."

I suddenly became suspicious as to what she might have planned. I was somewhat relieved that she showed *some* interest in addressing the issue, but based on her laissez-faire attitude, I had some questions.

"Who exactly will I be speaking to when I do visit?"

"Who would you like to speak to?" she replied in a sing-song voice.

Seriously, I had had enough with the games, the vague answers, the stupid questions.

"Obviously I want to speak to you! But I want to know if you planned to have anyone else there."

"mmmMMmmm," she replied again with that uneasy stomach-achy sound. "I wanted all of us to sit and talk."

I felt my heart start to pound and my head started to throb as I clenched my fist.

"What do you mean 'all of us?'" I surprised myself at the sudden loudness in my voice.

She hesitated, "Me, you, Pierre, and Troy. We can discuss it as a family."

"What? What does HE have to say to me? What does he have to say at all to excuse what he has done?!" My blood was at its boiling point. I had thoughts racing through my head of what he could have possibly said to her to make her think that a conversation could resolve this issue. "What in the world could he even say?!" I said aloud and into the phone.

"Well, I don't want to talk about that right now on the phone."

So we couldn't even have a conversation about the conversation we were planning to have.

"Okay. Goodbye," I said.

I was enraged. I wondered how she could be so casual and nonchalant about this. Even if he told her that I was crazy, or that I had made it up, how she could be so passive about it? I imagined there would be at least *some* emotion if you believed that your daughter had gone off the deep end, with no previous history of insanity. There were no follow-up questions; there was no urgency to get to the bottom of the situation.

"Goodbye. I love you."

"Goodbye," I responded. I couldn't say that I loved her at that moment. I couldn't even say that she loved me at that point. And hearing it didn't make me feel any comfort.

After that phone conversation, I realized that I had been given the answer I was seeking. Maybe it had been in front of me the whole time and I didn't want to see it. Daphne Baptiste was not ready or willing to give up her man for her children. It angered me, but more than anger, I felt disappointment to think that after such serious allegations, she would relinquish her role as a mother and continue to fulfill her role as a wife. It hurt me to know that instead of advocating for me, she chose to do so for him. Was it possible to continue to have a relationship with her after such a decision?

Through later conversations with Troy, it broke my heart to hear that at work she treated him like nothing more than a co-worker and associate, like a person who did not come from her own body. He worked the morning shift and she worked the night shift at the nursing home, and they often passed each other when her shift ended, and his began. They exchanged quick "hellos" occasionally when she wasn't feigning to be occupied or outwardly ignoring him.

One day Micah asked me, "Do you think your mom ever loved you?"

⚜

It was something I had never thought about. When she said hurtful things like "I can't wait until you get out of the house" or when she overly-criticized me, or worse, when she called me a "bitch," I excused it as a result of being overworked, or of hormonal changes due to her onset of menopause. I sat down with the photo albums that I had taken from my mother's closet and looked through the photos.

I paused at a photo of me holding up my hand with my fingers spread out, with a huge smile on my face. I was sitting next to a pink cake with a Barbie on it. It was my fifth birthday. I remember Mom used to make me a different Barbie cake every year for my birthday. She was wearing a big princess dress with individual, detailed pink swirls on it. I always looked forward to my birthday, just for that special cake.

I thought about the mornings when she would make me Cream of Wheat for breakfast and would put a smiley face of raisins in it, which I loved. I remembered the sound of her voice as she would sing to me, with a smile on her face.

You are my sunshine, my only sunshine. You make me happy when skies are gray. You'll never know thee, how much I love you. Please don't take my sunshine away.

I wondered if perhaps she simply became tired of me, and no longer wanted to make any sacrifices. Perhaps 25 years of motherhood was enough for her.

For the next month, I did not speak to my mother. She occasionally sent me texts saying, "how are you," or "how are you handling the heat" but her texts were ignored. I had no desire to engage in any superficial conversation with her. I felt that our relationship as mother and daughter, which was already fragile to begin with, was destroyed beyond repair.

I had helped Troy apply for financial aid for school now that he was away from home, but due to the fact that he was under the age of twenty-three, the state of New Jersey deemed him dependent, supposedly assuming that all students under twenty-three years of age get financial assistance from their parents. Unfortunately, because I was unemployed, I was unable to co-sign on a loan for him.

I had begun to feel helpless in assisting Troy, and continuing school became more of an "if" than a "when." Even a community college would be unaffordable without a loan. The army option came up again, simply for the purpose of continuing his education for no cost. Things had become desperate, and I ran out of plausible ideas for Troy to continue going to school.

In an unforeseen and incredibly generous gesture, Troy's new hosts offered to co-sign his school loan, but only if it was his last resort. First, Troy had to ask Mother.

The next day, with only two weeks left before the fall semester of his junior year, Troy ran into her at work on the elevator. He pushed the elevator button for the doors to close. Typically this elevator ride would have been in silence, but this time Troy broke the silence.

"Mom, I need a loan to go to school. Do you think you could please just agree to co-sign on a loan? You don't have to pay anything."

Her response: "I'm not doing anything until you move back into the house."

Troy looked at her intently and firmly stated, "I will not live under the same roof as that man. I don't know how you do it."

With that, the doors opened, and she walked out without saying another word, leaving him alone in the elevator. After that interaction, the final nail had been placed in Mother's coffin. She was no longer a mother. She was just a woman named Daphne.

I had given her enough benefit of the doubt. Assuming that I was actually crazy and delusional, one would imagine that a mother would at least be supportive, nurturing and try to find a way to heal her daughter. Not Daphne.

What struck me the most was not how Daphne reacted to me, but how she responded to Troy. She had no reason to treat him in the way she did. I truly felt that there was now a new responsibility bestowed upon me. Although I had always been involved as an older sister, there was no mother figure for him to fall back on. I was the closest person to my brother, and now I was fully responsible for him. He no longer had a mother, and I had to take her place.

20

Troy was calling.

"Hey, what's up?" I said as I picked up the phone.

"I just left Uncle Bobby's house."

"Awww, did you see the kids?" I really missed playing with my baby cousins and hearing their squeals of laughter.

"Yeah, they were excited to see me...I spoke to Uncle about what happened."

I took a deep breath and let out a sigh. I had not expected him to have that conversation during his visit. Rather, I had hoped he wouldn't have to.

"How did you approach him about it?"

"Actually, he approached me."

"REALLY?" I exclaimed, "How did he know?"

"Let me tell you the story, Cass!"

"Sorry, go ahead." My heart was pounding and I was becoming increasingly impatient. I knew that my disclosure wouldn't be contained for long, but I was extremely anxious about my family's reaction.

"He pulled me aside and told me that he knew what happened," Troy started, "And to be honest, I have a lot of respect for him because even though he's coming from the brother point of view—like me—and you'd think he'd automatically be-lieve his brother, he said, 'Only the two of them and God knows what really happened. I cannot pass judgment; Only God can do that.'"

"Wait...wait. How did he know what happened?"

"I guess either Pierre or Daphne told him."

I was baffled. I couldn't imagine Daphne saying anything, because she was more focused on keeping things quiet, and not even acknowledging the allegations. And I wouldn't imag-ine that Pierre would tell on himself. So it couldn't have been a matter-of-fact disclosure that I accused Pierre of molesting me; there had to be some sort of "explanation."

"What was the excuse they gave?" I asked. I braced myself for his response. I had come up with a few predictions prior to my disclosure, but now it was time to face the real outcome.

Troy sounded tentative, and he blurted, "They said that you made that up in order to move in with your boyfriend...Hey, it looks like rain!"

It took me a couple of seconds to comprehend what was just said to me.

"*That* is the excuse they gave?" I said. "What sense does that make for me to come up with something so serious just so I can move in with my boyfriend at the age of twenty-five? Are you kidding me?! And he believed that?"

I knew that he had no answers for the onslaught of ques-tions buzzing in my head, but I was ready to blow.

"I don't know Cassy, but I have to go; I'm driving," he said. "Just remember that their lies are expected."

"Okay. Drive safe. Bye."

Of course the lies were expected, but it was different know-ing that they were actually being absorbed by other people as the truth. To imagine, Pierre coming forward and saying non-chalantly, "Oh yeah, she accused me of touching her, but she just made that up so she could move in with her boyfriend." And people would really just eat that up? I couldn't get over it.

When Micah heard what had happened, he told me, "Well, they're only getting one side of the story. You're not there."

He was right. I had not given much thought to anyone else in the family besides my mother. I felt robbed of my ability to speak for myself, and certainly did not want the people I used to call parents representing me.

Thoughts were tumbling through my mind as I became increasingly angry. Over and over in my head, I kept thinking, *He's getting away with murder!* I imagined him going on with his daily routine, going to work, going home and getting dinner served by his wife, as if nothing had ever happened. It was something I had never thought about before.

I felt myself start to shake with fury. To imagine that he could sit there and paint me as a runaway child made me crazy. I don't know what angered me more: his lie or people believing it. I thought about taking him to court, getting him arrested, and punishing him for what he had done, but I knew that it wasn't an option.

Legally, I was past the statute of limitations, which means that I had taken too long to report the years of sexual abuse. If it takes a child more than five years to report sexual abuse, there can be no legal ramifications made against the perpetrator. Imagine: a five-year-old being repeatedly sexually abused by a person whom she is told to love and trust. If by ten years of age, she has not told anyone about the abuse, the perpetrator simply gets away with the traumatic licentiousness, as if it never happened.

It frustrated me that the law did not consider how young a child's mind is, or fragile it can be. In my quest to disclose my own story, I came across other stories.

One woman told me that she had been sexually abused by neighborhood boys at the age of seven. Another woman told me that she had gotten abused by her biological father but never dared to tell because he told her, "If you tell anyone, people will blame you," and she believed it. It was a secret that she kept buried inside of her out of shame and guilt, a secret she never intended to tell her family. Yet another woman who had never revealed this to anyone before divulged that she had been inappropriately fondled by her grandfather as a child. This was a secret she always kept for fear that her family would be shamed by such discovery.

It is not uncommon that a child directs any negative feelings toward her abuser inward—at herself—especially if the abuser is her caretaker. Consider that my abuser was the authority in the home, the one who set the rules, who determined the extent of my liberty, and the one who also provided me with food and shelter. He was also very highly revered by all other family members. Who could I have turned to without fear of repercussions? "Even at twenty-five, I was terrified, so one could imagine the terror of a fifteen-year-old or a ten-year-old, let alone a five-year-old."

I felt my blood burning and my head felt like it was filling up and expanding like a hot air balloon. I imagined going to the house, looking him in the eye and confronting him with all of my anger. I had an image of him sitting down, unfazed by the words that were coming out of my mouth and nonchalantly calling the police, having me arrested for something like trespassing.

No matter what I would say to them—"he molested me" or "he raped me"—it would result in no action. Instead, I would be the one taken away in the back of a police car like a criminal, while he sat on his throne in his home, untouched for his crimes.

During the day, Pierre's denial and Daphne's lack of a reaction to my disclosure implied that I had never been abused, but at night—when consciousness gave way to sleep—my brain vehemently persecuted me with scents, images, and pain as a reminder that it was real. Although I seemed able to manage my emotions during the day, they were coming out with a vengeance in my dreams. Almost every night, I had recurring dreams about confronting Pierre. Each night, the confrontation was different, and every time it ended with him attacking me, and me violently defending myself. When the dreams were not about confrontation, they were about him abusing and violating me all over again.

I dreamt that I had gotten a gig doing theatre and was invited back to New Jersey for a series of performances. During intermission, my mom called, asking if I was okay. I told her I was fine and that I was in Jersey. She started to whisper and urged that I come see her at the house immediately. I didn't hesitate; I ran as fast as I could out of the auditorium and to my house. The crunching of snow beneath my boots slowed as I reached the house.

Pierre was out front, trimming the hedges with a pair of loppers, and I caught a glimpse of my mother peering out the window. Pierre saw me and snickered, "You have some balls showing up here, you lying bitch."

I looked past him to my mother in the window, but she drew the curtains and stepped away.

"No point going inside," he snarled. "Nobody will listen to your stories. I'll make sure of that." A smile slithered across his face as he crept forward, brandishing the garden shears.

He lunged at me with the shears, but I parried the thrust with a side step, and then shoved him with all my might towards to the frozen ground. He landed face down in the snow with the garden shears lying next to him.

I grabbed the impromptu weapon, and when he got to his knees, I opened the shears wide and held them so the blades flanked his neck. I was going to end it—end him—like a weed, with one lop of the blades.

"How dare you. I think about what happened, and it hurts me every day," he whined, as crocodile tears slipped from one eye. He then swallowed deeply; his Adam's apple scraped against the blades, leaving behind tiny shaved hairs.

I felt tension build in my arms; they started to quiver like springs loaded with potential energy. I screamed—in anger, in pain, for it to be over, for him to be gone—and woke myself up.

Have you ever felt so much emotional pain that you would rather feel physical pain than feel what's destroying you from the inside out?

That morning, I lay in bed crying into my tear-soaked pillow and threw my fist repeatedly into the wall next to me, barely feeling the impact of my bony knuckles against the hard surface. I was sick of the nightmares. I was sick of the tears. I was sick of the unresolved pain I felt inside.

I had awoken Micah who immediately held me and tried to soothe me, wrapping his hand around my fist, restraining me from inflicting further pain on myself. Tears turned to violent sobs. There was no soothing what I felt inside. I felt unsupported by my mother, unprotected by the law, and immensely wronged with no solution to make it right. Deep down inside, I had been hoping that he would be punished, that he would be shunned from society—or at the very least, from my family—and would be punished to live the rest of his life alone and miserable to pay for what he did to me. Yet there was no one advocating for me but me.

I felt alone, as alone as I had felt at age five when no one knew what was happening to me behind closed doors. What made it worse is that even after I disclosed what happened, nothing changed. Aside from my brother, my family had vanished.

The recurring thought it my head was *it's as if nothing ever happened*. It had begun swirling in my mind like a mantra. What had been limited to my dreams began to permeate my woken state, causing me to experience flashbacks all over again. My lips inadvertently curled at foreign men with dark skin. I spontaneously experienced the pressure of his weight on my chest as I watched a movie in my living room. I had random images of his greasy face too close to mine, the feeling of his greedy hands on my skin. With each flashback, anger filled my soul like wine in a glass—I became drunk off of it, and reckless.

The next thing I chose to do, I am not proud of. It was a moment in which I felt cornered, vulnerable and was thirsty for revenge. I wanted him to feel the pain that I felt. I wanted him to lose sleep like I had. I wanted him to feel fear. I had crossed paths with a few shady people in my past, people who would not think twice to inflict pain on others.

I called an old friend and told him that a man had wronged me, and I wanted to send him a message. A few slashed tires and a good scare would satisfy me.

"Are you sure that this is what you want?" my old friend asked, "I know that you're not the type of person that requests these kinds of things. I have no problem doing it for you, but the question is: are you sure?"

I held the phone to my ear and hesitated. There I stood—a college graduate and an upstanding citizen—about to place an order as if I was on the line at McDonald's looking at the Dollar Menu. And as if on cue, my tears revealed my true emotion.

"What am I supposed to do?!" I yelled in between my sobs. For a person who once rarely cried, crying was becoming a pastime for me.

"Don't go down this path, because there is no undoing it once you do," he calmly replied.

I never thought I'd ever say these two words to this particular person, but I replied, "You're right."

I immediately regretted even making the phone call, ashamed of myself for temporarily losing my grip on my sanity. My solution was in front of me the entire time. I had to face them, both Pierre and Daphne, and say what I had to say and move forward, closing that chapter of my life. Clearly, my parents were set on living in their own fantasy, but I had the power to set things straight. I could not let this destroy my life any further.

I was not going to be treated as a runaway. I was going to confront him, face to face, and let everybody know who he really was. I immediately got on the computer and searched for cheap flights to New Jersey. I had saved up some money to hold me over until I found a job in Georgia, but I was willing to pay the $300 for the plane ticket to deal with this head-on. I was ready to fly to New Jersey and look the Devil straight in the eye.

I booked my flight and started drafting a letter. My plan was not only to confront him but to also inform the family directly about what had happened, as well as the decisions that I had made. They had a right to know the truth, and they would get it straight from me. I would not risk losing my extended family due to my parents' lies. My family had the right to make a sound decision with full knowledge of exactly what had transpired in our home for so many years.

I did not want my family to choose sides or to take any action; I simply wanted them to be cognizant. The social worker inside of me knew that things like this ought to be discussed out in the open and kept from behind closed doors. It's the only way to stop the perpetual cycle of sexual abuse.

It was also a preventative measure, so that when I would get married, I would have already made it clear that my parents were not a part of my life. My happiness on the big day would not be crippled by incessant questions about my parents' presence and involvement. I wrote:

Dear Family Member,

It is with great regret that I must be the bearer of bad news. I must inform you that the graduation party was not only in celebration of my graduation, but also a means for me to say goodbye to my family. I currently am living in Georgia, with my boyfriend.

This may come as a shock to you, but I have made multiple attempts to leave my house; this just happened to be the first successful one. I assure you that while I am content with living with my boyfriend, who I intend to marry, that was not the only reason for my departure.

My father, Pierre Baptiste, who you may already know is not my biological father, is a child sexual abuser and a pedophile. He started molesting me shortly after my brother was born and did not stop until 8 years later at the age of thirteen. My purpose in writing you is so that you may know the truth, regardless of what my parents may tell you.

I hope you realize that I had to wait until I was safely out of the home in order to disclose this information. I informed my mother on July 8th, 2011 and she continues to remain in the home with him, sleeping in the same bed, and cooking dinner for him as if nothing has happened, and as if he never robbed my innocence from me. Of course, this is not easy news to take, yet I do hope that as family, you support me enough to know that I would not create fallacies or excuses that are this grave.

What you chose to do or believe from this point forward is your choice, but my goal is to move forward and put this behind me and to start celebrating the life ahead of me. I hope that you will be a part of my future as well.

Pierre Baptiste is a sick man, and he will pay for what he did, if not on earth, than with what God has in store for him. After almost two years of therapy and one year of preparation, and unshakeable faith in God, I no longer fear him, nor do I fear any retaliation I may face for speaking the truth.

Although I am sending this letter to all of my family members, I would very much appreciate it if none of this is discussed with my grandma. She has always suspected that something has been wrong, but I'm afraid that the news is too heavy for her heart.

Again, I do regret being the bearer of bad news, but before you are subjected to lies, or half-truths, I am taking the opportunity to inform you of the truth.

Luke 12:2-3

"But there is nothing covered up that will not be revealed, and hidden that will not be known. Accordingly, whatever you have said in the dark will be heard in the light, and what you have whispered in the inner rooms will be proclaimed upon the housetops."

God Bless,

I made copies, and put each letter into an addressed envelope. Before I sealed them, I wondered what kind of a reaction I would get from mailing them out. I had texted a few family members for their mailing address, and one of the responses I got back was, "Are you sending good news?"

People were expecting engagement news and elegant invitations with ornate calligraphy, not a letter stating that I had been molested by a man they knew and loved. I thought about facing more rejection of the truth, anger and disapproval at sending the letter and making it public, or being shunned from people who didn't want to become involved.

I held the thick stack of envelopes in my hand and thought, "What greater rejection can I face than that of my own mother?"

The same way I was making concrete the finality of the relationship with my mother, perhaps this was an opportunity to do the same with my extended family. I wasn't expecting them to choose sides, or to take any action, but to simply read my letter and to understand. As I moved forward in my life, I wanted no questions or interventions about my decisions, and I wanted everyone to be aware of the facts.

✸

I watched from the window as my flight descended into Newark airport. I disembarked the plane and walked through the airport that I had been to so many times.

The smell of Jersey filled my nostrils—Indian curry, Italian spaghetti sauce, the sharp spice from African peppers. I smiled at the blend of foreign tongues speaking at once, enjoying the difference in cadence and intonation, music to my ears. As I sat on the train, I looked at the grayness of the concrete world, with bright graffiti colors on the walls and small bursts of green trees in between. It was odd visiting a place where I had lived for so long. It was such a foreign feeling knowing that I would only be spending a couple of days in a place that was so familiar. All I had with me was a half-filled book bag with some toiletries and a change of clothes.

I had planned to spend a total of four days. For the first two days, I would be visiting my brother, a few friends, and my cousins. The third day was reserved for D-day Part II. The last day was for travel.

I never would have foreseen the need for a second D-day, but as I walked off of the train at my stop, I knew that I had come on a mission, and I was focused on executing it. Only a handful of people knew I was going to be in town. Everything was planned out, and I couldn't afford any distractions.

D-day Part II was scheduled for Monday evening, promptly at 6:30pm. After visiting a few friends during my stay, I made the final social call Monday afternoon, with my baby cousins.

Troy and I stopped at their house. Marie opened the door with a huge grin, and when the door was open wide enough I heard a squeal as my two baby cousins ran to give me a hug. I had missed them so much, and they were thrilled to see me and my brother. I cordially greeted my aunt, whose raised eyebrows indicated surprise by my impromptu visit, but limited her reaction to a nonverbal one as she tersely said "Hello" while peeling vegetables at the kitchen sink for dinner. She had no idea why I was there and must've assumed that her husband would handle it when he got home. Troy and I boisterously played with the children, chasing them around, throwing them up into the air, while they squealed with joy. Marie looked on at us quizzically, wondering where I had gone, and if I would be staying for good. After about half an hour of play, my uncle pulled into the driveway from work at 6pm, as predicted. I had timed my visit perfectly.

"Cassandra!" he exclaimed. He wasn't expecting me.

"Hi, Uncle Bobby," I said with a smile. "Do you have anything planned right now?"

"No," he said cautiously. His answer didn't matter anyway.

"Let's take a ride," I said, smiling as I led him to the car.

"Where are we going?" he asked once he got into the back seat.

I turned from the front seat and said, "Home."

I'm pretty sure, at that moment, based on his facial expression, his heart plummeted into his stomach. We pulled out of the driveway, and I remember thinking that I had just kidnapped my own uncle, but he was a necessary component in my plan. My brother was there as support—for emotional support and for physically keeping me from gouging anyone's eyes out if it came to that.

Uncle Bobby was to serve as a neutral witness to what was about to transpire. I wanted him to see with his own eyes my confrontation with my parents and for him to come up with his own conclusion. I wanted him to hear the words that came out of my mouth, as I revealed details that I would have never known had I not been sexually abused.

This time, I had to bring out facts and show my true emotions. No holds barred. Evidently maintaining my composure on D-day proved to be ineffective. I needed to get a point across that I was serious and that this was not a phase or a joke that would blow over or disappear.

The ride would be fifteen minutes, and in that time, I thought I would familiarize myself with my uncle's thoughts on the matter, while my brother drove the car.

"So you've heard what happened, right?"

"Well...your father told me that you said that he did things to you so that you could move in with your boyfriend."

I turned and locked my eyes on his. "Now do you think, Uncle Bobby, that at the age of twenty-five, I need to come up with an excuse to move in with my boyfriend?"

"No. Of course not. But I know you're so smart, I don't understand why you didn't say anything when you were little... and why you'd wait until now."

"Who would I tell? My own mother doesn't believe me now; what would I have done when I was ten years old?"

He nodded with understanding, but started to defend my mother, saying, "Well...you don't know that she doesn't believe you..."

Any defense of my mother at this point was a trigger for my fury. "You have two young daughters at home. Don't tell me that if one of them came to you and told you that your wife had done this to her, you would continue to live as if nothing had happened and continue to be a husband to her."

"Hell no; I wouldn't even be able to stand the sight of her if my daughter told me that."

"You would *at least* investigate, ask more questions to see if it's true if there were some doubt. But from Daphne, nothing!

She doesn't even know where I live or where Troy lives, nor does she care!" My blood felt like it was speeding down the Jersey Turnpike at a hundred plus.

"Yeah, I understand what you're saying."

"Now, I get that this is your brother, but I just want you to be there so you can see what happens and make a decision for yourself."

"Whether he's my brother or not, that doesn't excuse him. When he's wrong, he's wrong." He paused, looked out the window, then returned to the conversation, "And don't do anything crazy. Let God do the judging. If he is guilty, his fate is already sealed. You don't need to do anything."

He had seen the anger in my eyes. From the tone in his voice, he was nervous. And although I had wanted to let my emotion show, it radiated off me and into the small car as if the heater was on full-blast. I had to take a few deep breaths as we drew nearer to the house; my heart was pounding and my sternum felt like it could no longer bridge the tension in my chest. I had to keep my emotion somewhat in check—I needed to focus on the points I wanted to make. I didn't want to become so overwhelmed that I couldn't effectively get my message across.

Alas, the deep breathing could not tame my fervent heart. We pulled up to the house, ready or not for whatever was to come.

21

⤫⤬⤫

I walked up the familiar walkway like I had hundreds of times before and rang the doorbell as a visitor. Behind me were my uncle and brother, but I made sure to stand where I could not be seen through the peep-hole.

"Who's there?" Pierre asked as I heard his footsteps come down the stairs.

I didn't reply.

The door opened, and as he laid his eyes on me, his eyelids retreated with desperation and revealed the stark whites of his eyes.

"Hello," he said, trying to sound casual.

I looked at him, knowing how terrified he must be, and walked past him into the house. I went straight upstairs to see where Daphne was. She was in her bedroom, with the TV on, blankets up to her chin.

It had been my assumption that she was still sleeping in the same bed as him, but the "mother defenders" wanted me to give her the benefit of the doubt, saying, "Well, you don't know if they're living as man and wife; she could be sleeping in your room."

Wrong.

"Hello," I said as I stood in the doorway to her bedroom.

"Oh, hello stranger," she replied, remote in hand. She didn't move a muscle. She didn't even flinch.

I waited for her to say something, do something, but she gave nothing. I took a deep sigh and turned away from her to explore the home.

I walked across the hall into my bedroom. The bed had been moved to the center of the room. The pillows were fluffed, and it was adorned with new, unfamiliar bedding that matched the drapes. Troy's room had also undergone renovation. It felt as if I had stepped into a bed and breakfast. *How odd*, I thought.

There was a plumber actively working under the sink in the hall bathroom, which my brother and I had once shared. The sink had been broken for as long as I could remember. The hot water would go from lukewarm to scalding hot in seconds, and my brother and I had simply become accustomed to constantly monitoring the temperature as we washed our faces or brushed our teeth. We had no choice, after many requests to our parents to fix it. *How odd.*

I walked into the living room and gathered all of my pictures. I remembered looking at them when I was moving out, contemplating whether I should take them or not. Part of me had wanted to have mercy on my mother. Since I had taken all of my baby pictures and photo albums, I thought it would be fair to at least leave my framed communion picture, a picture from the prom, and a graduation picture. Now, there would be no mercy. I unzipped my half-empty book bag and collected every single picture of me and my brother from that living room. I felt nothing.

Pierre stood only a few yards away in the dining room, observing my actions, and didn't speak one word to me. I think he knew better. He engaged in casual conversation with my uncle as if it was a social call, and my brother loomed in the background. As a 5'11" young man, he couldn't be missed, but it was evident that Pierre was avoiding him.

Once I had finished packing up, I realized that my mother hadn't even left her room. I returned to the doorway of her bedroom, where she continued to lay.

"You're not getting up?" I asked, bewildered. She hadn't moved an inch.

"Well I have work tonight, and you came here so unexpected. You know I have to sleep."

I didn't think that I needed to provide my mother with a reason to get out of bed. One would think that simply being her daughter would be enough. Clearly it wasn't.

"Well, you said you didn't want to talk on the phone, so I'm here live and in the flesh, and I'm ready to talk."

I felt the irritated tone of my own voice like sandpaper in my throat. I thought that I was keeping it together quite well, yet internally, I was infuriated. I sat on a plane for three hours to have this conversation, but she was uninterested. Obviously she wasn't sleeping, so her excuse was bullshit. Again, I walked away.

There was an awkward moment where Pierre, my uncle, and my brother lingered around in the living room, unsure of what was to happen next.

"Mom, let's go! The sooner you get up, the sooner you can go back to sleep," I yelled down the hallway.

Begrudgingly, she walked out into the living room, arms crossed, brows furrowed, like a petulant teen. For a moment, everyone stood in the living room, awkwardly shifting their weight, fidgeting with their hands, shifting their eyes around the room.

"Tell them what you want," Troy said, nudging me.

I paused, feeling somewhat awkward that I now had the floor and everyone's eyes were on me, questioning.

"I'm calling a meeting. We all need to sit down and talk."

Daphne immediately voiced her complaints, "You barge in here, so bold and demanding, and expect people to just stop what they are doing..."

"Oh, I'm sorry; did you need the prep-time to make some tea?" The sharpness of my tongue was unexpected, both for me and for my mother, as she just looked at me in shock. No one was going to deter what I was ready to say.

Pierre was the farthest from me in the group, standing in the hallway, attempting to disappear within the shadows, seemingly absorbed with his cell phone, with his neck bent, staring at the small screen.

"Well, you guys go ahead with your meeting...I'm busy."

I called his bluff. "Everyone, including YOU, is going to be in this meeting," I replied, putting emphasis on every syllable, looking him directly in the eye. I don't believe I had ever spoken to him in that manner before in my life.

On his face, I saw the urge to reprimand me for speaking to him like that, but he thought against it as he nervously returned attention to his phone.

"Well, we can't meet, the plumber is here," he said in Creole.

"Outside," I said with a shrug.

Obviously he did not want the plumber to overhear our family discussion. I couldn't care less where we met, or whether the plumber heard or not. Those details were insignificant. I just wanted to get it over with.

"Well, someone has to stay with the plumber."

Was I the only one seeing that this guy was avoiding this meeting like the plague?

"I'll stay with the plumber," my uncle volunteered.

"Nobody needs to stay with the plumber—he'll be fine." I had made the executive decision. "So let's go meet in the porch."

In his one last attempt at avoiding this confrontation, Pierre said, "I need to make a quick phone call. I'll be right there."

I rolled my eyes.

"Fine," he conceded, and he reluctantly filed out the door and into the porch with everyone else.

I stood front and center with my back to the door that led to the backyard. Perhaps it was my training as a therapist kicking in: in a potentially hostile situation, always position oneself near the closest exit. Daphne sat opposite from me, arms crossed. My uncle sat to the right of her, leaning on the side of the porch. Pierre took a seat the furthest from everyone, isolated in the back, to the left of my mother. Troy took his stance to the right of me, leaning against the house door, arms crossed.

At that point, my heart was thumping wildly, as if I had just sprinted a few miles at the track. My hands were shaking, despite my holding them together for stability. When I first spoke, my voice was shaky. I had no idea how this would turn out, but I was here, and everyone was gathered, ready to hear what I had to say.

"So," I said, trying to keep my voice steady and my emotions at bay, "I heard that you guys are saying I ran away to be with my boyfriend?"

That came out so much weaker than I thought. Just like D-Day Part I, I felt again like a small child. Nobody responded, just submitted blank stares. I looked at my brother, almost for help—like he could provide me with the words. He tilted his head as if to say, "Go on and say it."

I shifted the weight on my feet and tried again. I decided to address a specific person, instead of speaking to everyone at once.

"Mom, I told you what happened before I left, right?"

"Yes," she responded nervously.

"What did I say?"

"You said that Pierre touched you inappropriately," she said as she looked back at him.

He was staring at his phone.

"And...?"

She looked to him to answer that question, "He said..." she started, as she turned to look in his direction, searching for an answer.

He continued her statement, still pecking at his phone, "How could I have done something like that?"

Obviously that wasn't a yes or no answer; however, I had come prepared for that—and for him. I reached into my bag and pulled out a Bible.

I put my right hand on it and stated, "You are a child abuser and a pedophile. You molested me, and I swear on this Bible that what I say is the truth, or may God strike me down where I stand. I want you to swear on this Bible that you did not do anything to me."

I stepped past my mother and held out the Bible for him to take, waiting for his next move, daring him to take it, daring him to swear, knowing what a superstitious person he is. I stood there with my arm fully extended. The Bible was less than a foot away from his face, and the weight of the hardcover text felt like redress on my fingertips.

"I don't need to do that," he responded indignantly, regarding the Bible as if it carried some deadly pathogen.

My arm remained outstretched, with the Bible lingering in the air, challenging him. After a few seconds of a standstill, Mother reached out and took the Bible from my hand, placing it in his lap.

"Swear on the Bible," she said.

Everyone's eyes were on him.

He brushed the back of his left hand quickly across the Bible and hastily said, "I didn't do what she said."

Surprisingly, Mother persisted before I could contest, "No, you have to say exactly what she said."

Pierre looked at my mother with confusion, like a mutt on the first day of obedience training. He raised his left hand slowly and placed on the face of the Bible.

"I did not do those things you said I did...In the name of God."

"Wow," I said, shocked at his gall and arrogance. "There is a special place in Hell for you...And you wonder why you're going blind! God has a plan for you!" I guess I had underestimated him as the scum of the earth.

"I've had glaucoma for years," he shrugged.

"Exactly," I replied. As far as I was concerned, spiritually, his fate was sealed.

"The things that you were studying in school have just made you crazy. You've just lost your mind," he exclaimed.

As those words escaped his mouth, everything seemed to slow down. I had to blink; my vision had become blurry. I was suddenly distracted by a pounding in my ears; I could feel the blood rushing to my head. I felt clammy and wiped my sweaty palms on my pants. My mouth, on the other hand, had stopped producing saliva, and when I tried to swallow it felt like I was pushing gravel down my throat. Meanwhile, he had continued to speak, but I could not hear him. It was like I was wearing earmuffs, dampening the sounds coming from his mouth.

All I could process was that he had called me crazy. And from the dreams that I'd been having, being called crazy resulted in gory violence towards Pierre. I took a deep breath and looked again at my brother, who stood stoically in the corner. Again, with his eyes he told me to continue. I told myself that this was not the time to go crazy. I had much to say, and I needed to be composed to express myself. I had to focus.

"Okay. You want to say that I'm crazy," I said as I wrung my hands, cracking my knuckles one at a time. "If you didn't do anything to me, how would I know where you keep your pornography collection?" I trudged forward.

"Oh yeah? Where do I keep it?" he replied, challenging me with a smug look on his face.

"Right under the TV in your cabinet...and in your closet."

I realized much later that I didn't even need to answer the question because by simply asking me "where," he already confirmed that he did indeed possess pornographic movies. And yet, there was no reaction from Daphne. Her face remained expressionless. I directed my next statement at her.

"Do you remember when I fainted in church? He laughed at that and said he thought I was pregnant."

Her eyes widened as she protested, "But you were only a little kid."

I wanted to bang my head against the wall. Did she not get the memo about the fact that he was a pedophile?! That means that he was a predator, who preyed on young children. He preyed on me.

I was appalled at her ignorance.

"And you didn't do anything to protect me *at all!*"

"*Me?*" She responded. The look on her face was that of a woman who was not involved in the situation at all, as if she were an innocent bystander. "What could I have done? I go to work every night!"

"And when you found my bra in your bed, you didn't think to do anything then!"

"What..." she started, "I did laundry for the whole family, so there was no issue to have your bra in the room."

I let out a maniacal laugh. It was hilarious to me that she was in complete and utter denial. I could do nothing else but laugh, because there was no logic present. I started to wonder if this was real, or if it was another dream. I felt like I was on the Truman show, and the people in front of me were just paid actors.

"Explain to me how I would know that you did not have sex with your husband for two years? How would I know that?!"

At this point, I wasn't looking for a response, and she had none to give.

"You know what?" I said. My eyes locked onto her; I had forgotten that anyone else was in the room. All I saw was the woman who was supposed to be my mother, sitting in front of me with an expressionless face, irritated about not being in bed and watching TV.

"I want nothing to do with you," I said. "From what you've shown me, you are not a mother. You mean absolutely nothing to my life. You are a disappointment..."

Although she sat there, staring at me blankly, apparently Pierre felt the need to jump in.

"Hey! Don't you disrespect your mother like that!"

What happened next had to be conveyed to me by my brother. Something in my brain finally snapped, and I blacked out completely. Something triggered me to explode, like I never had before in my entire life. All of the rage that was building inside of me for months—for *years*—finally found its way out.

I propelled my fist into the one of the doors, breaking the glass, screaming at the top of my lungs. I kicked the door in, sending splinters of wood through the air, and then turned toward the vile predator who was supposed to be my father.

"I'll kill you! I'll kill you!" I screamed, pointing at him with my bloodied hand. "I know where you work and I know people who will take care of you—or better yet, I'll let my lawyers come down on you and you can have the same things done to you in prison as you did to me."

Troy wrapped his hands around my waist, lifted me up, and carried me down the steps to the back yard.

All I saw was the blurry green grass. I gripped the fence tightly and hunched over gasping for air. My hands quaked and I was panting loudly as hot tears and blood from my knuckles dripped onto the grass.

Uncle Bobby had come outside to speak to me, and I can only assume that it was to try to calm me down; I heard nothing that he was saying. I heard sounds coming out of his mouth, but I could not make out any words. I looked at him, perplexed, as my breathing steadied, and then started pacing in the backyard before I kicked another porch window.

Troy had gone inside to talk to Pierre and Daphne. My mind was racing, and my hands were still trembling. Troy walked out of the porch and handed me my belongings. It was time to go.

"You're dead to me," I yelled as Uncle Bobby and Troy walked me to the car.

My insides were on fire. I felt like I had swallowed burning coals and they were simmering my insides. I took deep breaths and shifted in the passenger seat, but nothing alleviated the pain in my stomach. I was perturbed by the intensity of the burn, as if my anger had manifested into flames and was consuming me from the inside out. I promised myself that I would never allow myself to feel such an intense emotion again.

As we drove away, my uncle leaned forward and said to me, "I understand what you are saying. His body language said everything—He was afraid of you."

I felt relief, that I at least accomplished my mission. I said what needed to be said, and my uncle saw the truth with his own eyes.

I replied, "Because he knows what he did. If you were accused of rape, how would you react?"

"I'd be so angry they would have to have the police hold me back from the person who accused me of something I didn't do." Uncle Bobby shook his head. "*He* just sat there."

"As a matter of fact," my brother interjected, "he had much more of a reaction about me not telling him what was in my mail! He almost got into a physical fight with me over that, but today he wouldn't move an inch from his seat."

We discussed what each of us saw from our individual perspectives, and Troy disclosed his own conversation he had with Daphne while my uncle was attempting to console me outside.

He said, "I stood in front of her and told her, 'I almost didn't go to school because of this' and she just looked at me and said, 'That's not my problem.'"

At that point, I was beyond feeling any kind of shock about Daphne's behaviors. Nothing that she said or did meant anything to me anymore, and I hoped Troy received his closure as well. During the ride back to my uncle's house, my uncle expressed fear of me making Pierre's actions public, or taking him to court. "When you have a bundle of grapes and one grape is sour, you assume that all of the grapes are sour. He is my brother, so I don't want people to judge me because I have two little girls."

I assured him that no one would judge him for the actions of his brother. Yet I was unsure if I wanted to take Pierre to court. Court would require money, energy, and time, which at that exact moment, dealing with the simmering charcoal in my stomach, I wasn't sure I wanted to dedicate to him.

When I returned to Georgia, I nursed my battered, swollen knuckles and processed my visit to Jersey. The physical burning sensation in my stomach had ceased, but I still felt a burning rage in my heart. I had many sleepless nights, and the violent, gory nightmares resumed. I felt that I accomplished everything that I wanted during my visit, yet I still felt so empty and unfulfilled.

I was still processing his audacity to hold the Bible in his hands. I was processing my mother's calm demeanor while I slammed the undeniable truth in her face. But my next step was to wait; I waited for the reaction from my extended family to the letters I made sure to mail out before my flight home. I felt that I should be nervous, but I was so numb from my interaction with my so-called parents that I didn't feel anything. I re-read a journal entry that I had written about my hesitation to send the letters:

This morning I addressed & stuffed envelopes for family members to receive the letter I drafted. I feel torn about sending them. What was my purpose in sending them? Is it a good idea or bad idea? Right or wrong? I don't want to do things out of vengeance only. Part of me wants to expose him for what he is and make him suffer. Part of me doesn't want to keep quiet anymore and so I deserve to set the record straight and defend myself. Is that being selfish or doing what's right? Then I question whether I should have faith in God and Karma or if I should take my future into my own hands. People won't know what hit them. People don't want to hear bad news, or about child molestation—they want celebrations and good news. But I am constantly reminded of Teti's words, "You lived it, so they can hear it."

22

ver the next two weeks, responses from family members started to trickle in like rain in a Georgia summer. First, my cousin Melissa called and told me I was brave for standing up and finally speaking out. Moreover, she said that she'd be more than willing to point me in the right direct for legal counsel since she was in law school. Only a few days later, my cousin James called. He said he remembered me telling him once that my dad used to watch movies with him at night when everyone was asleep when we were kids. He said he was shocked, but without a doubt, he believed me. Then an aunt, who seemed quite uncomfortable discussing the matter, called and said that she'd keep me in her prayers. Overall, her contact was awkward and limited, but I supposed that I couldn't expect everyone to take the news well.

One day, another cousin called. He said that he couldn't believe that my father—the uncle that this cousin looked up to—was capable of the things I'd accused him of.

"He just doesn't seem like the kind of person—"

"Please," I interrupted, "Tell me what a pedophile is supposed to look like." I felt my skin turn flush. I was over it, over everyone trying to tell me what a pedophile was or was not. "Is he supposed to have claws and fangs and linger in the shadows on rooftops? Bishop Long—have you heard of him?"

The line was quiet.

"Hello?"

"Yes—yes, I've heard of him."

It didn't matter if he'd answered or not; I kept on: "Bishop Eddie Long is a 'normal looking' man who preaches the word of God to hundreds of people, tells them how to be true Christians. And how about Jerry Sandusky? He was a highly revered and respected football coach at Penn State. Wouldn't you know it— both were accused of sexual abuse."

Again, the line was silent but for a long sigh. "Look," he started, "I'm sorry but—"

"Don't even say it," I snapped. "You don't have to believe me, but don't insult me by defending a man that you don't really know." I hung up the phone. This was harder than I thought.

After that, responses flooded in; some by phone, some via e-mail. Some expressed shock and doubt, others shock and support. Some reprimanded me for waiting so long to tell, others commended me for my courage. After speaking to my cousin, however, I decided to respond to the reactions slowly and deliberately, one at a time.

I was at Wal-Mart, standing in line at the cashier's checkout, when my phone rang. It was an unfamiliar number with a New York area code. I sighed and let the call go to voicemail. *Here we go again*, I thought.

When I got into my car, I pressed '1' to check my messages.

"Hello, Cass-honey. This is your Tati Nancy," she said in her Haitian accent. "I know it's been a while since we last spoke, but I have to tell you: I believe you! I believe you, honey!" Her voice started to tremble. "I'm so sorry that you had to go through that—that he made you go through that."

I let out the breath that I'd been holding as I listened to her words.

She continued, "Know that I'm here for you, dear. Know that I love you. Please call. Bye."

For the first time I can remember, tears slid down my cheeks and they felt good. All I kept thinking was: *She loves me! She cares about me!* I was so overjoyed. Simply hearing the emotion in her voice was all I'd been craving the whole time—someone to understand. She felt for me and believed me. I was so happy that I was actually smiling and crying; it was truly a bizarre feeling. I couldn't help but laugh at what it must've looked like.

It felt amazing to feel loved. It reminded me of Micah's reaction after my disclosure to him. It reminded me of Troy's support. I sat and cried and cried in my car in the parking lot of Wal-Mart before I called her back to let her know how much I appreciated her support, and how she had no idea how much it meant to me. She expressed how she wished she could've been there to help me as a child, and I told her that she couldn't blame herself. We both cried together. Before saying goodbye, I expressed my endless gratitude.

She responded, "That's what family is for."

The phrase lingered over the line for some time. My definition of family was no longer the same as the rest of the world. As I hung up the phone, I knew that I did have a family, real family who stood by me and cared about me.

There was another person, however, who I could not tell in a letter. Although my stepsister Sorelle and I weren't particularly close, we still had a relationship that I wanted to grow. In order for that to happen, I needed to be forthcoming with her about why Troy and I abruptly moved. Furthermore, I didn't know what Pierre may have done to her on her visits to our house, and perhaps by telling her about my disclosure, she could find the courage to divulge any abuse she may have experienced.

After a lengthy text conversation, she asked that I call her; it was her lunch break. I had just walked into the laundromat delicately balancing the phone between my head and my shoulder, while carrying a laundry basket and detergent. After answering many questions, I finally shared with her the truth about why Troy and I had moved out of the home. At first, she was quiet.

"Are you okay?" I asked. Clearly this was not easy news to take.

As the conversation fell into silence, the humming and clattering of the laundromat's machines stole my attention.

"I knew it."

"I'm sorry...what?" That wasn't the answer I was expecting. Was she molested too? What did she mean by that?

"I didn't know it was him specifically," she started.

I put the final coins in the washing machine, and stepped outside to hear clearly what she had to say.

"My aunt is a person who is known for sort of predicting things and seeing things in her dreams. She said that a father-figure in my life, she didn't know who, may do something inappropriate to me. So ever since I was young, I was taught to watch out for things like that. She was right about the father figure, but she was wrong about the target. Instead of me, it was you."

"Wow," I said as I hung on to her every word. "So, he never put his hands on you?" I clarified.

"No. I don't know if you noticed but I didn't visit often when I was younger. My mom didn't trust him. He had to fight my mom to get me to come over."

I felt relieved that she hadn't been touched by him. I do have memories of Sorelle coming over when we lived in Philly, but only for a few days at a time, perhaps only once a year.

"Why didn't your mom trust him?" My curiosity piqued.

"Well, this might sound weird, but when he asked my mom to marry him, he said that he had to first go to Haiti to get permission from the Devil through a voodoo ceremony and she wanted absolutely no part in it." She continued, "So every time I came to visit, my mother told me 'pray before you eat, after you eat, before you walk into a room, pray before you do anything.'"

My brain flooded with the information she provided me. I had judged my sister early on as a religious fanatic, as a "holier-than-thou" type of person, due to first impressions of constant prayer and constant talk about God. I immediately wrote her off as judgmental and unapproachable.

I now realized that I had misjudged her. What I had not known was that she was merely following the instruction of her mother and protecting herself from the evil of her father.

As for her reports of him doing voodoo, I was not surprised. I had always wondered what caused Pierre and Sorelle's mother to separate, but I hadn't expected that to be the reason.

I said aloud, "I never understood why a man would abandon his responsibility to one child, and then take the responsibility of another only one year later. We are only one year apart."

"I don't know all of the details. But my mother told me that he had something to do with the separation of your mom and biological father," she said.

"All I know is that she left my father, and that she and Pierre lived in the same apartment building. I had no idea why she left him," I replied.

We continued our discussion, speculating, asking questions, and expressing our feelings to one another. She was supportive to me, and I was supportive to her. It was then that I made the decision to move beyond my initial judgment and started to see her as a more approachable and down to earth person. I was happy that our relationship, in time, would be given the opportunity to develop.

In the end, I was satisfied with the decisions I had made to tell my family, and I felt ready to move forward with a clear mind. I was no longer alone, and I felt free of my silent burden.

Then one night, I had another terrible dream, but this time it was not about Pierre. I was in the kitchen, searching for something to eat in the fridge. I sensed a presence in the room, and I got a sudden urge to turn around. Across from me stood my mother, her face expressionless.

"Hey, Mom" I said in a casual tone.

"Hey." Her response was flat, emotionless.

I shut the fridge door behind me despite my growling stomach. "Mom, you know what Dad did to me. You know what happened." I pleaded.

"No," she muttered in a barely audible voice. I didn't even see her lips move. Her eyes stayed fixed, in a zombie-like stare.

"Mom? Mom!" I yelled. I wanted to wake her from this trance she was in. "You know I wouldn't make this up. Open your eyes. I know you know the truth." I approached her to put a comforting hand on her shoulder.

"No!" It was more of a growl than a word. Her eyes quickly darted to my hand on her shoulder. She had grabbed a knife from the kitchen table, swung, and nicked my arm with the blade.

I quickly withdrew my arm, putting pressure on the spot where beads of blood had started to form. I looked up at her wild-eyed screaming, *"What are you doing?"*

Her face had contorted into a grimace. She had taken a wide stance, an attacking position. She had the same look in her eyes that you saw in the eyes of a rabid dog on the street. Before I could protest, she leapt forward. I caught her arm midair, wrestled the knife from her hand, and with one swift move—before I could even think—I severed her hand from her body with the sharp blade.

She gasped, crouching on the floor, covered in blood. Her eyes had transformed to those of a wounded child. She looked up at me questioningly, with tears in her eyes, perplexed by why I had attacked her. "I'm your mother," she whispered.

I awoke feeling dreadful, more so than with any of my violent nightmares of Pierre. I felt sick to my stomach. All types of thoughts flooded my head, and I felt tremendous guilt.

I challenged myself to think as a social worker: would I have treated my mother the same if I were her therapist instead of her daughter?

No, if she were my client, I would empower her, encourage her. Perhaps she was depressed and felt hopeless, unmotivated and alone. Unfortunately, I was not mentally or emotionally prepared to do that for her. Yet as a social worker would do, since I could not personally provide the service, I found resources that would be able to provide that service for her. I enlisted the help of one of my most supportive aunts.

I expressed my concerns to my aunt, and asked that she look after my mother. Maybe she could confide in my aunt and find strength through that relationship. I didn't want my mother to feel abandoned, as much as it irritated me that she had abandoned me. I still cared for her.

23

As far as I was concerned, I had disclosed to everyone that needed to know. Yet I constantly struggled with the decision to keep my grandmother in the dark. She held a very special place in my heart, and at 83 years old, I was extremely protective over her. She was also particularly sensitive for me, having me in her custody for my first few years of life.

For the most part, I didn't want to upset her. I knew the news would be heart breaking, and I didn't want to hurt her. I had no doubt that she would believe me, causing there to be a rift between her and my mother. As ironic as it was, a small part of me wanted to allow my mother to continue to have the support of her own mother in her life.

A few months after the disclosure, my grandparents came to the United States for their usual visit. I had already informed my grandma during her last stay that I had plans to move in with my boyfriend, yet my grandparents were completely shocked and unprepared to discover that Troy had moved out of the home as well.

Immediately, suspicions fell on my parents. It was odd that both children would spontaneously up and leave their parents. I called the house every Friday to talk to my grandmother, taking advantage of not having to incur long-distance fees while she was in the country. That was the day that Daphne was guaranteed to be out of the home, at her part-time day job. My brother also visited every Friday for approximately an hour to spend time with our grandparents.

It was evident that my brother and I were avoiding my parents. My grandmother initially started with questions like, "Have you called your mom?" Unsatisfied with vague answers, she gradually became more direct, and persistent, asking, "What made your brother leave?"

I gave her a half-truth: "He's going to school." My grandmother was a smart woman, knowing that it was something more. I led her to believe her assumption that Pierre's strictness was what drove Troy and me away.

It was hard not being fully truthful to her, but the most I told her was, "There are things that happened in the home that you wouldn't be pleased to hear about, so please leave it alone." She respected my wishes, but reported feeling uneasy at the home.

"I don't know if I want to come back here," she told me during one of our conversations. My parents worked during the day, leaving grandma and grandpa alone in the home. They did not speak one word of English, and couldn't walk anywhere even if they wanted to, as the nearest store was over one mile away from the home.

When my parents did return from work, they retreated to their room. "We really come here to see you. It makes me so sad that you and your brother are not here," she explained. She often called me, describing the meals she was preparing, wishing that she could send some to me. My brother was also heartbroken by the separation. After one of Troy's visits, my grandfather held on to my brother and pleaded, "Please, don't go. Don't leave me."

My grandparents returned to Haiti, still unaware of the details related to the tension in the family. My grandfather, who already had a negative relationship with my Pierre due to money management, disliked him even more due to his suspicions that he pushed my brother and me out of the home. As much as my heart ached that my grandparents returned to Haiti without me seeing them, I felt relieved that since they were so far away from the drama, I wouldn't have to explain the situation.

Months went by, and I spoke to my grandparents regularly. I missed them tremendously and wanted to see them in person, but for the time being all I had was the phone. I had gotten engaged, and Grandma was the first call that I made. She was thrilled about the wedding, which Micah and I had decided would take place at the shores of Labadie, Haiti via a five-day family cruise.

"Will your parents be there?" she asked.

I hesitated before answering, "I don't know."

"By the way you're answering it sounds like you haven't asked them," my grandmother deduced.

I didn't know how to respond. I thought by now she understood that my parents and I weren't on talking terms.

"No, I haven't asked them, because I know they won't be coming."

There was sadness in her voice as she let out a sigh like a deflating balloon.

"This has gone too far," she said, "The family should not be separated like this. If they are not coming, I'm sorry but I won't be coming."

I was silent. I felt a pain go through my body as she uttered those words.

"I know that you want me to be there, and this may be hard for you to accept, but I'm sorry I will not be able to be there. To imagine being in attendance, without your parents there, having to explain to the family, it would be too uncomfortable. I would end up making myself sick from crying so much."

I kept my voice steady, stating, "But Grandma, you are not coming to the wedding for my parents, you are coming for me. I personally am requesting for you to be there."

"I'm sorry, but if your parents can't be there, then I won't be able to make it," she said more firmly than before.

"But you need to be there!" I yelled. Tears began flowing from my eyes, "You are like a mother to me."

"Don't cry. You'll make me cry. But it's time that issue gets resolved. You need to go and ask your parents for forgiveness for whatever you did to them. You need to take a flight out there and stand before your parents, and plead for them to pardon you."

"Grandma!"

It was hard to interrupt her once she got going. When she started talking, it was as if she stopped listening.

"You don't understand what has gone on in that house! And I told you before that I can't tell you the details because it's too much for you to handle!" At this point, I was at a full-fledged cry. I continued, "It is their choice to not to be a part of my life. Mom has abandoned both Troy and me. She doesn't know where either of us lives, nor does she care. We had to struggle to find a way to get him to continue to go to school. She doesn't care! If you knew what happened, you would say it is she who should ask *me* for an apology!"

My grandmother gasped. "And there lies the problem. How could a parent have to apologize to a child? It's because you think like an American and that once you reach eighteen, you don't need to respect your parents. But you must remember that the fifth commandment says 'Honor thy parents' and no matter what you should respect that. It is a mother who risks dying for her child in childbirth. A child never dies for a mother. Pride is one of the deadly sins. You cannot allow yourself to be so prideful, demanding apologies."

I didn't have a response for her. I started to become angry, but I could only be angry with myself for keeping her in the dark. At times I held my breath and bit my tongue, keeping my anger inside.

"You know I never envisioned that this family would end up like this. It's sad because my neighbors ask about the family, and I don't dare tell them what's been going on. I have pictures of you as a baby taking your first step, taking a ride on your little car. When you would cry, and your mother wasn't there, I gave you my own breast to soothe you. And to now hear that this family is in such disarray, it breaks my heart. Satan has entered that home."

It made me sad to hear her speak like this. She reminded me of the extended periods of time that my mother was not there to raise me, milestones missed. Again, I informed her, "You have no idea what has gone on in that house."

"Of course I know what went on," she started. "Pierre was far too strict on you, and he was overbearing, always asking you questions and demanding things of you. It got to the point where you and Troy couldn't take it anymore and you left."

"Grandma!" I had to yell in order to get her attention. I had to interrupt her. "What you must understand is that this is not over something petty like discipline. You have your own experience and you know that Mom will stand by her husband, right or wrong, over her own children or parents. The problem is Pierre. He is an evil man. *He* is Satan. He wasn't a disciplinarian, he abused me."

I could hear the air rush into her lungs as my grandmother gasped again. "You said what?"

I hesitated. I quickly went through the things I had said to her. I then questioned the meaning of "he abused me." In English, if a person said something along the lines of "my parents abused me," there are three possible options: sexual, emotional or physical. Translated in Creole, my grandmother on the other end of the phone understood it as only one thing: sexual abuse. I remained quiet on the other end, with tears streaming down my face.

"You said he abused you?" she exclaimed.

I quietly replied, "Yes."

I had just inadvertently disclosed to my grandmother that I had been abused by my stepfather as a child. It was not my plan to reveal the truth to her at all, especially not over the phone, with her over a thousand miles away, unable to console her.

She was surprised but maintained her composure. She asked the expected questions: "How old," "How long," and "why didn't you tell earlier?" By now, after being assailed with the questions of relatives, the answers came easily. She was gravely disappointed in my mother, and was concerned about which family members knew. The conversation lasted for three hours. I answered the rest of her questions, stressing that I would not go into specific details. She decided that she would keep this from grandpa, since he already had serious issues with Pierre.

Although she seemed to have taken it well, as a therapist, I knew that some things may take time to manifest. I advised her to make an herbal tea, or a home remedy, which my grandmother was known for, in order to handle the emotional shock. I proceeded to call her every day after that for a few days. All I could think of was my grandma having a heart attack because of me.

She reported occasional tears, but overall she had taken it well. She continued to ask more questions, which I answered, leaving out the uncomfortable details. She was upset that she had trusted Pierre, and wanted to confront my mother about her decisions. I told her that Pierre was a great actor, and she should not blame herself for trusting him. I asked her not to confront Mother for two reasons: First, it wouldn't make a difference and second, Pierre still had access to their money, and I didn't want her to risk the possibility that he would punish her by abusing his access.

Grandma finally agreed to going on the cruise for the wedding, relieved that she wouldn't need to explain anything to other family members. And my Christian grandmother even gave me the perfect excuse to give those who were not "in the know." She stated, "Pierre is ill, and your mother chose to stay with him." Once again, my grandmother was my best friend, and there were no more awkward conversations between the two of us.

24

I found myself exasperated by some family members' requests for me not to prosecute him. For some people it was to not draw negative attention to the family. For others, it was more of a spiritual reaction, focusing on the repercussion from a higher power. "God will judge him." What angered me was the idea that such hush-hush behaviors are most likely what perpetuate the cycle of sexual abuse. Keeping quiet not only protects the predator who may potentially abuse again but also keeps the family ignorant and in the dark about the reality of sexual abuse.

Pedophiles do not only exist on the news or on *Law & Order*. They exist in our everyday lives as our neighbors, our teachers, our friends and family members. These predators are not the dark and scary monsters or the "Boogey Man" that are on children's cartoons or scary movies. Child sexual abuse is not limited to older men abusing young girls. Women are abusers also. There are men who abuse young boys and women who abuse young girls. There are children abused by older children. As Pierre often told me, "Education is key." Both children and adults need to know.

I did consider pursuing legal action against Pierre. I did some research and found that although I could not have him criminally prosecuted, I could involve him in a civil suit in which I could sue him for at the least the cost of my therapy. Due to the criminal statute of limitations, a prosecution for a crime must be commenced within five years after it is committed. This meant that Pierre would not spend one day in jail for the crimes he committed against me. But, I could make him pay.

According to the National conference of State Legislatures:

> *"[M]any states allow civil actions for cases involving sexual abuse of children. By the time the victim discovers the sexual abuse or the relationship of the conduct to the injuries, the ordinary time limitation may have expired. This 'delayed discovery' may be due to emotional and psychological trauma and is often accompanied by repression of the memory of abuse. Child victims frequently do not discover the relationship of their psychological injuries to the abuse until well into adulthood—usually during the course of psychological counseling or therapy. They may not even discover the fact of such abuse until they undergo such therapy."*

According to their website (www.ncsl.org), various states had different statutes of limitation for civil suits. For many states, their statutes expired after as little as two years.

Other states caught my attention. Connecticut allows action within 30 years from the date the victim reaches "the age of majority." In New Jersey, actions can be initiated within two years of the date of "reasonable discovery" of the "injury and its causal relationship to sexual abuse." In Pennsylvania, the statute of limitation was 12 years from the date of a victim reaching his or her age of majority (eighteen years old).

Technically, since the abuse started in Pennsylvania, at the age of twenty-five, I could file a civil suit against Pierre. But how much energy was I willing to exert? How much money and time was I willing to burn to drag him into court? I felt that I was searching for an official "win," something to replace the lack of support by my mother. I needed someone to validate me and acknowledge the injustices against me. This is when I decided that my way of winning would be to succeed in educating the public about predators like Pierre.

I've had my conversations with God, asking Him, "Why me?"

After much searching, I found my answer. It would become my quest to stop child sexual abuse by increasing awareness. Its effects are devastating, and our society will continue to suffer the repercussions of child sexual abuse without increased awareness and advocacy.

Here is what I think many abused men and women would say if they had the platform to express themselves:

I am the person you call an addict, a druggie, a crack head or pothead. I may be the homeless person you step over on the street or your co-worker who seems fully functioning. I didn't wake up one day and decide that's what I wanted to become. But drugs for me are an escape from the pain that I feel inside. Getting high or drunk makes me numb and helps me forget the fact that my uncle took advantage of me every time he was charged to "babysit" me. To this day, I have yet to ever utter that fact to anyone aloud. I feel ashamed and dirty, and the drugs help me take care of those feelings.

I am the person you call a prostitute, a whore or a slut. I've been taught since I was a child by my mother that I am only good for my body, so graduating high school wasn't a crucial part of my life plan. I had a dream of becoming a doctor, but that dream was lost once mother dearest started bringing Johns to the house for me to service. She was always pretty liberal with the belt, or shoe, or whatever was within reach, threatening to beat me if I ever told anyone what went on in our own home. I was not to air our "dirty laundry" because it's how I had food in my belly. This is the life I know, and the life I live.

I am the person you call a loner, "emotionally-unavailable." Simply put, I don't trust. I can't trust. Life has taught me at an early age that I can't rely on people who I'm "supposed to." My grandfather molested me and my two sisters. My mom was an alcoholic and didn't believe me when I told her. I never told anyone at school. How could I breach the topic? People in school didn't pay much attention to me. I made sure to get great grades, join the school marching band, and become president of the chess club. The kids they paid the most attention to were the ones doing drugs or getting detention. I couldn't tell anyone what was happening at home because I didn't want to be a "bad kid." I was a perfectionist. Plus, if I did tell, that would mean my sisters and I would be placed in foster homes, maybe even separated, and I couldn't risk that. Now as an adult, I have two dogs who are loyal and they can never break my heart.

I am the person you call the life of the party, the risk-taker, the daredevil. I laugh in the face of danger. I have anonymous sex, and I travel alone late at night. I can't allow what happened to me in my past stop me from doing things that I want. My next-door neighbor, a kid only a few years older than me, made me do things against my will. I thought he was my friend but clearly he wasn't. Now I don't really give a shit and live life as I want.

I am the person you label a pedophile. I was molested for years by a friend of the family, and now I find it difficult to resist my attraction to young children. It's a way of power, and control. I know that it's wrong and I try not to act on my sexual feelings, but it's what I was taught. I can't help who I've become.

We are all products of society. We are the results of negligent parents, lack of education, and the perpetual shame that surrounds sexual abuse.

⸎

My dream is to one day run a non-profit organization for the treatment of both children and adult survivors of sexual abuse. I envision a coalition of people who go out to schools, churches, and various locations to educate children and their parents about sexual abuse. Even if a child is not being sexually abused, simply presenting a child with an environment of open communication about the matter makes it easier to discuss it with other people, such as a friend, a teacher, a counselor, or their parent in the event that it does occur in the future. Children would be more willing to breach the topic: "Remember the people that were here talking about good touches and bad touches?..." Proper education and resources for the parents prepare the parents for such discussion.

I dream of a place where children can come with their families and have family therapy to address the trauma that has not only affected the child, but the family as a whole. Parents and family members may feel guilty or responsible, not knowing how to help the family move forward. Perhaps they are still in denial.

There would be an art therapist and play therapist on staff, assisting children in expressing their trauma and pain. Often, children who are abused tend to have difficulty verbally expressing their thoughts and emotions. The body's natural reaction as a form of protection is to shut itself down, making trauma work that much more delicate, requiring tact and skill. Both art and play therapy will help facilitate the processing of the abuse.

On staff, there would also be a couples therapist to deal with impact of child sexual abuse of adult survivors in intimate relationships. The therapist will assist the disclosure of abuse to the significant other and provide education to the significant other about the effects of sexual abuse on adult survivors. After being violated, there is a serious fear of intimacy and sometimes confusion about healthy boundaries. Both partners will have to explore comfortable techniques and understand triggers for the adult survivor.

Overall, my dream is to have resources for the prevention of sexual abuse and for the treatment of trauma from sexual abuse, from childhood to adulthood. My dream is to increase awareness about sexual abuse and to decrease its frequency in the United States by changing the culture of shame and guilt.

In the end, do I regret my disclosure? Not one minute of it. Certainly, it was an emotional roller coaster with highly stressful moments, but I have never been at a happier place in my life. Emotions come more readily to the surface than they have in the past, and although I may be inclined to call myself a "crybaby," I am embracing the emotions as they course through my body. It feels liberating to no longer suppress my true feelings.

I currently live with my fiancé and love of my life, Micah. I have fostered my own individual relationship with different members of my family, which has caused a great increase in communication, in comparison to the very infrequent contacts when I was living with my parents. I enjoy a new and great relationship with my sister, and we become closer every day. I have developed a wonderful relationship with my future in-laws, who have accepted me into their family with open arms. I view Micah's mother as my own, and her infinite love and wisdom has been uplifting. The physical distance between my friends and I has not changed our relationships, which are kept alive and in some cases even stronger through regular phone conversations. I have been blessed in finding many unexpectedly supportive and loving people in my journey. I have a renewed faith and a stronger relationship with God. I have transitioned from the girl who kept everything in, carrying her own burdens, solo, to a person liberated, living her life to the fullest, truthfully, without lies or cover-ups. I refuse to bury any longer.

As for my mother, I still struggle with the emotions I feel towards her. It's amazing how despite the fact that she was not the one who abused me, the pain that she has caused me has been unbearable. The anger has subsided, but it will take years for the disappointment to go away and for the forgiveness to set in. Her betrayal towards me is second only to the sexual abuse as one of the worst things that's happened in my life. Do I think that she is an evil person? No. I believe that she was once a loving and emotionally invested mother. She cared for me and nurtured me. She was the woman who walked over to my elementary school and yelled at the aide for not properly looking after me when another child pushed me to the ground.

Unfortunately, somewhere along the way, my mother got lost as a parent and needs some time to find her way again. She made the conscious decision to sever ties with her daughter. I believe that she knows in her heart what truly transpired, but she cannot face the harsh reality. I don't believe than anyone can help find her but herself. My mother did not respond well to my aunt or any other family members reaching out to her. If they breached the subject about sexual abuse, she would either avoid their calls or texts, or flat out say that she did not want to speak of it, for fear of getting *madichon*. If she ever makes a turn around, will I be ready with open arms? There is no way of knowing. I will spare myself the pain of hopeful wishing.

As for Pierre, there is no doubt that he is a very sick individual. Yet, he was the man who introduced me to music, encouraged me to get good grades, and was the main parental figure while my mother was working hard. I have moved beyond vengeance for him. I know that the knowledge of his exposure is tearing him up inside. His glaucoma has gone into over-drive, and he frequents Haiti to perform voodoo ceremonies with hopes that he will get better. I have washed my hands of him and I am moving forward with my life, and I'm not looking back. It is up to him to find peace and ask God for forgiveness. I have found my peace.

My brother has been blessed, living with the loving and supportive family that he's with, who have also become like family to me. He no longer works at the same job, and is still estranged from our parents. He is excelling academically and pursuing a career as a police officer and detective. I continue to look out for him, as I always have, and I always will. I know that despite this drastic change in his life, he has a bright future ahead of him.

In this experience, the negative pieces in my life have been removed and replaced by positive ones. This certainly has been a growing experience for me, and I am a new and improved individual. Life is much clearer, and things actually feel real.

I hope that my story encourages men and women across the country to muster up the courage to tell their story. Even if not to disclose to friends or family, at least tell a therapist. The road is not an easy one, but from my personal experience, it has been worthwhile. There will be confusion, anger, tears, screams, anxiety, and even hopelessness, but in the end it will be worth it because you will be free of your burden, free to live the life you want to live, free to live without fear, and free to be your true self. Telling may not only save you, but it may save another victim, who is waiting to be saved by your bravery.

Child Help USA: National Child Abuse Hotline
1.800.4.A.CHILD (1.800.422.4453). No caller ID used.
Reporting and victim-related resources. Spanish available.
www.childhelpusa.org

National Center for Mental Health Services
1.800.789.2647 U.S. Dept. of Health and Human Services
national referral database. Spanish available.
http://mentalhealth.samhsa.gov/databases

National Runaway Switchboard
1.800.RUNAWAY (1.800.786.2929). No Caller ID used.
Resources for runaways and family members.
Spanish available. www.1800runaway.org

National Suicide Prevention Lifeline
1.800.273.TALK (1.800.273.8255)
Support for suicide risk or mental health crisis.
Spanish available. www.suicidepreventionlifeline.org

National Domestic Violence Hotline
1.800.799.SAFE (1.800.799.7233). No Caller ID used.
National call center refers to local resources. Spanish plus 160
other languages available. www.ndvh.org

Rape, Abuse & Incest National Network (RAINN)
1.800.656.HOPE (1.800.656.4673)
Routes to your closest Sex Assault Crisis Center.
Spanish available. www.rainn.org

Darkness to Light
1-866-FOR-LIGHT (866-367-5444)
Darkness to Light provides a toll-free number for individuals
living in the United States who need local information and resources about sexual abuse. Any individual, child or adult who
needs resources about sexual abuse can call the Helpline.